Movements of Grace

"It is refreshing to find a Christian who works passionately with adolescent youth (in 'Reality Ministries,' which he founded and leads) and who, at the same time, engages passionately with deep, serious theology (Barth, Bonhoeffer, the Torrances, and others). While I have some questions about Jeff McSwain's super-gracious convictions, I have no questions about his profound immersion in the main Christian questions."

—FREDERICK DALE BRUNER
author of *Matthew: A Commentary*

"An eloquent and compelling exploration of the reality of God's grace in Christ Jesus, this book is a must-read for anyone who wants to grapple with the full extent of what Jesus' humanity means for our humanity, our discipleship, our prayers, and our proclamation of the gospel . . . In the process, he shows us that we can fully, freely, and joyfully respond to God because we are God's beloved children, thanks to the mediating role of Christ and the gift of the Spirit. This is theology at once profoundly gracious and immensely practical."

—KRISTEN DEEDE JOHNSON
author of *Theology, Political Theory, and Pluralism: Beyond Tolerance and Difference*

"American Christians, both Protestant and Catholic, have much to learn from Karl Barth and the Torrances. Jeff McSwain has been transformed by Christo-realism and is taking it to the streets and youth of Durham, North Carolina. I recommend this book as an entry point into a much-needed understanding of the gospel."

—CHRISTIAN SMITH
author of *What is a Person? Rethinking Humanity, Social Life, and the Moral Good from the Person Up*

Movements of Grace

The Dynamic Christo-realism of Barth, Bonhoeffer, and the Torrances

JEFF MCSWAIN

WITH A FOREWORD BY JEREMY BEGBIE

WIPF & STOCK · Eugene, Oregon

MOVEMENTS OF GRACE
The Dynamic Christo-realism of Barth, Bonhoeffer, and the Torrances

Wipf & Stock
An Imprint of Wipf and Stock Publishers
199 W. 8th Ave., Suite 3
Eugene, OR 97401
www.wipfandstock.com

ISBN 13: 978-1-60899-630-8

Manufactured in the U.S.A.

Grateful acknowledgment is made for permission to reprint previously published material:

Scripture quotations, unless otherwise indicated, are taken from the Holy Bible, New International Version®, NIV®. Copyright © 1973, 1987, 1984 by Biblica, Inc.™ Used by permission of Zondervan. All rights reserved worldwide. www.zondervan.com.

Scripture quotations marked JBP are taken from The New Testament in Modern English, revised edition, © 1958, 1960, 1972 by J. B. Phillips and 1947, 1952, 1955, 1957 by Macmillan Publishing Company. Used by permission. All rights reserved.

Scripture quotations marked NRSV are taken from the New Revised Standard Version Bible, copyright © 1989 by the Division of Christian Education of the National Council of the Churches of Christ in the United States of America. Used by permission. All rights reserved.

Scripture quotations marked RSV are taken from the Revised Standard Version of the Bible, © 1952 [2nd edition, 1971] by the Division of Christian Education of the National Council of the Churches of Christ in the United States of America. Used by permission. All rights reserved.

Excerpts from Church Dogmatics by Karl Barth. Copyright © 1936–77 by T. & T. Clark. Reproduced by kind permission of Continuum International Publishing Group.

Excerpts from The Cost of Discipleship by Dietrich Bonhoeffer. Copyright © 1959 by SCM. Reprinted by permission of Hymns Ancient & Modern Ltd.

Excerpts from Ethics by Dietrich Bonhoeffer. Copyright © 1955 by SCM. Reprinted by permission of Hymns Ancient & Modern Ltd.

Excerpts from Worship, Community, and the Triune God of Grace by James B. Torrance. Copyright © 1996 by Paternoster. Reprinted by permission of Authentic Media Limited.

Excerpts from The Mediation of Christ, revised edition, by Thomas F. Torrance. Copyright © 1992 by Helmers & Howard. Reprinted by permission of Helmers & Howard.

Excerpts from Space, Time and Resurrection by Thomas F. Torrance. Copyright © 1976 by T. & T. Clark. Reproduced by kind permission of Continuum International Publishing Group.

This book is dedicated to my mentor and friend Alan Torrance, who, in Scripture and in life, has shown me how to trust the indicatives of grace.

"Not that I have already obtained this or have already reached the goal; but I press on to make it my own, because Christ Jesus has made me his own." (Phil 3:12 NRSV)

Contents

Foreword

A PASTOR WAS OFTEN found staring at a train that ran past his Church every morning. Asked why he found it so compelling to watch, he replied: "It's the only thing in my parish that I don't have to start and push."

This book responds to a sad distortion of the Christian faith, one that is all too common: we turn the Gospel into something we are convinced needs to be activated and kept in motion by us, something that in the last resort (despite all our talk of "grace") we have to make happen. Jeff McSwain points us unerringly to the joyful alternative, that the momentum behind the Gospel has been running before any human decision, underway long before any of us were born, eternally in motion even before the creation of the world. The utterly dependable love of God, the ceaseless giving and giving back of the Father and Son in the Spirit—this precedes all our willing and acting. And into this extraordinary divine dynamic we are invited. We are not summoned to make it happen, but because it is already happening.

Jeff eloquently expounds the ways in which this momentum engages our lives, drawing on the trinitarian wisdom of the Torrances, Dietrich Bonhoeffer, and Karl Barth. He throws into relief the astonishing freedom generated by God's "movements of grace." There is the freedom of knowing "we are not thrown back on ourselves" (as Jeff's teacher, James Torrance used to say). In these pages we cannot miss the huge stress on the "alreadyness" of the Gospel: that Christ—the incarnate, crucified and risen Son—has already provided the perfect human response that we could never provide, already shunned the temptation we could never resist, already pleaded the prayer we could never utter, already defeated the fear we could never conquer. Our own response now is enfolded into his prior response on our behalf. In the words of Jeff's mentor Alan Torrance, "grace is a yes to a yes."

Not only freedom *from*, but also freedom *for*—as Jeff shows so clearly, the Gospel's liberation brings not passive acquiescence, nor cringing obedience, but a life in the Spirit re-shaped and energized by Jesus himself, the only fully human being. To share in Christ's human response on our behalf is not to be de-humanized but *re*-humanized. This is just what is so remarkably embodied in Jeff's extraordinary initiative among young persons at risk in Durham, North Carolina. Those of us who have experienced Reality Ministries at firsthand will never forget it. Here is a youth initiative that is propelled by news of a God of utter solidarity, a God who identifies with those who believe they deserve nothing and find in Christ they are given everything. Jeff and those who work with him never try to compel young people into a response of faith, yet paradoxically, just because of that, the responses come, and in ways that surpass expectation and transform lives irreversibly.

This, then, is not a book of "academic theology" in the abstract and negative sense. Though rooted in years of study and research, and alert to the nuances of trinitarian doctrine past and present, these words have not emerged from some safe place of refuge, apart from the struggles of faith. They have been tried and tested in the midst of often bleak and unpromising circumstances, where the future has often seemed fearful and daunting, and where the word of the cross has sometimes felt hopelessly weak. But the testimony of these pages is that whenever Christ the High Priest is at work, by his Spirit an unstoppable movement of grace is unleashed, so that the lame will dance and the mute will sing.

Jeremy Begbie
Duke University

Preface

THIS BOOK BUILDS ON several pieces written while at the University of St. Andrews, Scotland. I am grateful to have had the opportunity to sit under Jeremy Begbie, Steven Guthrie, Trevor Hart, and especially Alan Torrance, to whom this book is dedicated. Resident lecturer Richard Bauckham, along with guests Colin Gunton, Murray Rae, and Iain Torrance, enriched my experience at St. Andrews.

One of the formative highlights of my time in St. Andrews was the weekly gathering at the Canlises' home, where my wife Susan and I met to bat around theological ideas with Matt and Julie, Kristen Deede Johnson, and Stephanie Mar Smith. We formed a tight bond with other friends studying at St. Andrews. Thank you, Bruce and JJ Hansen, Tim and Sarah Gombis, Ross and Lauren Blackburn, Steve and Julie Guthrie, and Matt Jenson.

I am grateful to others who had major roles in my theological education leading up to St. Andrews: Gordon Fee, whose biblical interpretation class at Regent College exploded my biblical foundationalism; Charles MacKenzie at Reformed Theological Seminary, an inspirational expert on Blaise Pascal and the first teacher to give me an appreciation for the love going on between the Triune Persons; and Gary Deddo, whose teaching through Fuller Theological Seminary gave me a new pair of glasses for understanding the person and work of Jesus Christ.

Here in Durham I have had wonderful friends with whom to talk theology, beginning with my original coffee shop mates Douglas Campbell and Christian Smith. Alan Koeneke, Cleve May, Dave Hunsicker, Zac Slay, Brad Turnage, Cameron Boltes, Steve Larson, and my faithful friend and pastor Allan Poole have also been great partners on this theological journey.

I am deeply grateful to my editor Carol Shoun, whose kindness and expertise blessed me in the preparation of my first book.

Finally, I must give special acknowledgement to my family. First, to Susan and our children, Emily, Caroline, Malissa, and David. Because of the love we have shared as a married couple and as a family, I am more deeply aware of the reality of God's love in which we participate. Second, to my parents, Mal and Wanda McSwain, who taught me and continually remind me that we really can trust the picture of God that we see revealed in Jesus Christ, "the visible expression of the invisible God" (Col 1:15 JBP).

Jeff McSwain
Durham, North Carolina
June 2010

Abbreviations

BQ	*Baptist Quarterly*
CD	*Church Dogmatics*. Karl Barth. Edited by G. W. Bromiley and T. F. Torrance. Translated by G. T. Thomson et al. Edinburgh: T. & T. Clark, 1936–77
EvQ	*Evangelical Quarterly*
ExpTim	*Expository Times*
Inst.	*Institutes of the Christian Religion*. John Calvin. Edited by J. T. McNeill. Translated by Ford Lewis Battles. 2 vols. Library of Christian Classics (LCC). Philadelphia: Westminster, 1960
JBP	*The New Testament in Modern English*, J. B. Phillips
JSNTSup	Journal for the Study of the New Testament: Supplement Series
ModT	*Modern Theology*
NRSV	New Revised Standard Version
OS	*Ioannis Calvini opera selecta*. Edited by Peter Barth et al. 5 vols. Munich: C. Kaiser, 1926–52
RefR	*Reformed Review*
RSV	Revised Standard Version
SJT	*Scottish Journal of Theology*

Introduction

Awakening to Grace as Reality

TEN YEARS AGO THE penny dropped, and I was changed. Instead of holding to the belief that I had brought Christ into my life, I began to see that my life has always been in his. Since that day I have incessantly marveled over this newfound awareness of God's grace. And it all happened during a systematic theology course at Daytona Beach! Our professor pulled back the curtain of the Reformation to trace the church's christological heritage, beginning with the patristics, traveling through John Calvin, and on to Karl Barth, before coming full circle to be tied most profoundly to the patristics in the work of Scottish theologian T. F. Torrance.

During the course, a couple of transformational concepts began to take shape in me: the eternal connection of the Father, Son, and Spirit—most notably, the oneness of being between the Father and the Son—and the mind-blowing realization of the oneness of the Son with fallen humanity in the grace of our Lord and Savior Jesus Christ.

To think that our Holy God would condescend in love to embrace humanity at its worst in order to rescue us from sin, death, and the devil and to reconstitute the personhood of all men and women, equipping us to share in the life of the Triune Persons—that was a truth that at once exposed, scandalized, and blessed me. I remember walking along the crowded beach after class and resonating with the words of the Apostle Paul: "From now on we look at no one from a human point of view." Later, I tried to recapture my experience in a poem:

Flesh and Truth at the Beach

O Son of Man, My Brother
Did you, in your judgment of grace,
    trump Adam's flesh by embracing it?
I believe

O Lover of My Soul
Did you, in becoming a man and even the Man
    take on flesh exactly like mine and even mine?
I believe

O Consuming Fire
Did you, in your incarnate passion,
    make war and make new my flesh,
    nailing the old to its final place?
I believe

O Risen Shepherd
Did you, in gathering us all in yourself,
    bring us home,
    where we share your life with the Others?
I believe

As I walk out on this beach,
    skin glistening as far as the eye can see
    I'm in awe

You became one with us all,
    and then . . .
Bone of our bone
Flesh of our flesh
True God of true God,
You put us in the truth

Beach brothers and sisters,
can you believe it?!!!

For my years of Christian ministry before January 2000, I habitually proclaimed the gospel in a way that undervalued the union of Jesus Christ with both God and humanity. On the one hand, while I paid lip service to the fact of Christ being God, my articulated theory of the atonement defied it. I portrayed a God who sent Christ to assume the world's sin so that God could stay pure in himself. As the rationale went, sin separates us from God, so Christ had to be separated from God in order to pay the penalty for our sin and to protect God from it. It did not dawn on me that I was pulling apart the inseparable and eternal relationship of Father and Son in order to explain how a Holy God could deal with sin without touching it. The language of God sending Christ without the equally important biblical language of Christ coming on his own initiative caused me to think of Christ more as the object than as the subject of the atonement.

On the other hand, my expressed belief in (or again, at least lip service to) the fact that Jesus Christ was God kept me from understanding the fullness of his humanity. I thought of him as the object of my worship but never as the subject who himself believed in God and served God while also struggling mightily against the constant temptations that we all face in our human condition. Thus paradoxically, in similar fashion to my underrepresentation of Christ as the subject who acts from the God side, I was neglecting to give Christ his proper place as the subject who acts from the human side. In refusing to define both God and humanity by Jesus Christ, I was not giving full play to the mediatorship of the one who was and is as fully man as he is fully God. To say it another way, by compromising the subject status of Christ from the God side and the human side, I was short-circuiting the gospel of grace, which premises God on both sides!

A year and a half after my beach experience I found myself on another shore, the east coast of Scotland, at the University of St. Andrews. I had arranged to take a study leave from ministry, to spend a year immersed in Scripture and in the theological pursuit of Christology. Indelibly printed in my memory is the day, early on in my master's program, when I left Alan Torrance's office and took a long stroll, contemplating his remarkable assertion that "grace is a yes to a yes." One might say that Alan's phrase aptly describes my theological project over the last ten years, and I feel as though I am only beginning to apprehend the depths of his comment.

To Barth, Bonhoeffer, and the Torrances, grace is not an abstract truth; it is reality itself. By God's revelation in Jesus Christ we are given the blessed assurance to know that all human beings are included in the humanity of the Savior. And in Christ we discover the movements of grace, a God-humanward and human-Godward double movement, all by the Holy Spirit. These theologians were keen to remind us that Christ's ongoing mediatorship includes all appropriate human responses to God. In fact, only by grace and in union with Christ do we have true response-ability. It is this "going with the flow" of the Holy Spirit *en Christo* that makes Christo-realism so dynamic and life-giving.

I don't provide detailed summaries of the theologies of these men; this book is meant to introduce the reader to the operating framework of grace in their thought. Having come to Barth through the Torrances, I will attempt to bring the reader along the same road. It is my hope that with Barth, Bonhoeffer, and the Torrances we will better grasp how wide and long and high and deep is the love of God and more readily see and experience true human life in its God-created glory and God-given direction—from the Son to the Father by the Holy Spirit.

Chapter 1

Introduction

Ambassadors of Reconciliation

Thomas F. Torrance (d. 2007) completed his PhD, *The Doctrine of Grace in the Apostolic Fathers*, under Karl Barth after the war (1946). He, along with Geoffrey Bromiley, was the editor for Barth's *Church Dogmatics* as translated into English. Perhaps Torrance's greatest contribution to theological studies was his penchant for transcending the East-West divide in the church by pulling together common themes in sources otherwise found under the unfortunate rubrics of "Catholic" and "Protestant." Much of Torrance's work is founded on his patristic heroes, notably Irenaeus, Athanasius, Cyril of Alexandria, and the Cappadocian fathers. With his acute knowledge of pre- and post-Reformation theology, Torrance, unlike many Calvinists, is able to properly contextualize Calvin as standing on the shoulders of these patristic predecessors, especially when it comes to Christ's solidarity with all of humanity.

James B. Torrance (d. 2003) was also a student of Barth, and with his older brother he contributed mightily to the field of Calvin studies. Like Tom at Edinburgh, James spent years at Edinburgh and Aberdeen teaching a thoroughly Reformed brand of theology that was nevertheless by its very nature ecumenical. Together the Torrances articulated tirelessly how God in holy love created every human being for filial purposes and how, because God loves us more than he loves himself, God pursues us in the Spirit, giving himself to re-create us in the Son and to reconcile everyone to the Father. Because we belong to God by virtue of creation and redemption, taught the Torrances, trying to live for ourselves is an exercise in futility.

While under the supervision of James's son, Professor Alan Torrance, at St. Andrews, I had the pleasure of getting to know James and his wife, Mary. Happy memories abound from my times in James and Mary's parlor, sipping tea and talking theology. Of all the things we discussed, the phrase that has stuck with me most poignantly is James's saying "We must give everyone his humanity." What did he mean? That we must recognize in every person his or her true humanity as it is defined by Christ—his or her union with the Son of Man Jesus Christ, in the way Paul sets it forth in Colossians 1, Romans 5, 2 Corinthians 5, etc. Every one of us must be defined, not by our Christian action or inaction, but first and foremost by our ontological solidarity with the Second Adam. And we would never want to give Adam more effective influence over the human race than Christ!

It was this theological perspective that gave James not a little influence with leaders in the South African church when it came to the struggle against apartheid. As ambassadors of reconciliation, the Torrances passionately believed that we must always begin with the end in mind. We move *from* reconciliation to reconciliation. Not only are we all reconciled to God; we are all ultimately reconciled to each other. That is the unavoidable reality. We can either go along with this economy of grace, learning to be "eschatological activists,"[1] or we can resist it, bringing destructive consequences to our relationships with God and one another. Compelled by Christ's love, we preach the good news so that all might freely choose to live into the reality of God's love for every human being: You *are* reconciled to God, and so, we beseech you, on behalf of Christ, *be* reconciled to God. . . . Do not receive the grace of God in vain. . . . Today is the day of salvation! (2 Cor 5:18—6:2).

My introduction to the writings of the Torrances was Tom's *The Mediation of Christ*. I am not sure if it was the difficulty of the content, my lack of an appropriate interpretive framework, or just the need to get used to Torrance's complex writing style, but I found reading the first part of the volume much like being on a train screeching slowly out of the station. However, once I began to catch the clickety-clack of the Torrance rhythm, my train ride turned into an exhilarating adventure across the landscape of God's grace. Again, regaining the ontological

1. A phrase borrowed from two of my other St. Andrews mentors, Trevor Hart and Richard Bauckham. See *Hope Against Hope: Christian Eschatology in Contemporary Context*. As complementary to the themes of my book, I also recommend Bauckham's *God Crucified* and Hart's *Faith Thinking*, along with two of Hart's essays, "Humankind in Christ and Christ in Humankind: Salvation as Participation in Our Substitute in the Theology of John Calvin" and "Irenaeus, Recapitulation and Physical Redemption."

perspective of the Fathers, Tom is always helping us to think of God's relationship to humanity within the framework of the wondrous exchange articulated by Calvin and derived from Irenaeus and Athanasius: "This is the wonderful exchange which out of his boundless kindness he has entered into with us: by becoming Son of Man with us he has made us sons of God with him."[2]

For the Torrances, as we shall see, this exchange involves much more than a simple transfer of static properties, for *being* and *act* are constantly interpenetrating one another, and the divorce of the two can be nothing short of disastrous for the church. For example, we would not want to speak of being made one with Christ as daughters and sons of God without giving proper attention to Christ "becoming sin" and the Son of Man's death and resurrection for our sakes; we would not want to preach a message of the world's salvation that is "soft on sin" or did not call people to repentance or could not be refused (as in universalism or other determinist constructs); and finally, we would not want to fall prey to an overrealized eschatology that does not account for the prevalence of evil in a redeemed universe.

It is the concept of evangelical repentance, derived from Calvin, that helps us to move past potential gnostic or dualist tendencies. The connection of this concept to Barth's teaching that humanity must hear God's "No" to sin inside God's "Yes" to humanity is hard to miss. For in the statement "Father, forgive them; for they know not what they do" (Luke 23:34 RSV), spoken to those immediately present and to all of us whose sins put Christ on the cross, we can hear God's indictment against our sinfulness in the context of his overall affirmation of us. In order to avoid a conditional gospel, the Torrances insist with Calvin and Barth that we must preach about sin only as the implicit back side of a positive statement. To do otherwise is to risk making grace the exception to the rule—an exception applicable to us only when certain conditions are met—at which point grace is no longer grace![3]

2. Calvin, *Institutes* 4.17.2, quoted by T. F. Torrance, *Trinitarian Faith*, 179. Cf. two other versions of this truth: from Irenaeus, "Out of his measureless love our Lord Jesus Christ has become what we are in order to make us what he is himself" (*Against Heresies* 5 pref., quoted by T. F. Torrance, ibid.); and from Athanasius, "God became man so that man might become God" (*On the Incarnation* 54).

3. Someone might object that, contra the theologians above, Paul preaches the bad news first in Romans 1–3. Douglas Campbell's monumental work *The Deliverance of God* (Eerdmans, 2009) has recently provided a clear understanding of how to read and

However, as we come to understand who Christ is and the hypostatic union intrinsic to his person, we will begin to grasp, by the Holy Spirit, the onto-relational dynamic of Christ's life and, by God's grace, our own. In response to God's unconditional love will learn how to be people of gratitude in the midst of our broken lives, people of hope in the midst of our fallen world. We will learn to walk by faith and not by sight, all the while assured that we are indeed "hidden with Christ in God."

Much credit is owed to Tom for courageously reintroducing the ancient concept of *theosis* to Protestants. Recognizing *theosis* for what it is and what it isn't provides us a trinitarian basis for proclamation and an epistemological capacity for response that maximizes the place of the Holy Spirit in evangelism. It has been my experience that, yes indeed, *theosis* will preach!

I hope that the following chapter will provide a good entry point to the Torrances, so that readers will find their hearts singing with the good news that truly is good news. The Torrances surpass even Barth in their emphasis on the ongoing vicarious humanity and high priesthood of Christ, and the effect is to give us a fresh impetus to preach the gospel in Christ so that others might receive it in Christ.

---

interpret Romans retrospectively, demonstrating how Paul always wants to preach and receive the gospel from solution to plight, not the other way around.

CHAPTER 1

Preaching Jesus Christ as the Gospel of Grace and the Ground of Faith

A View from the Evangelical Theology of T. F. and J. B. Torrance

JESUS CHRIST IS THE gospel. This pithy phrase is echoed by many in the Protestant evangelical world, but rarely understood in all its fullness. Undoubtedly Jesus Christ is who the gospel is all about; through him we receive grace. Yet what about the idea that Jesus Christ *is* grace in his person? It is my purpose in this chapter to unpack this loaded statement and to apprehend the riches of the grace that is Christ Jesus. Few in recent years have done more to focus our attention on the idea that Jesus Christ is the embodiment of grace than the brothers T. F. and J. B. Torrance.[1] We will turn to the Torrances at every point in our journey as we seek to grasp the meaning inherent in the concept that Jesus Christ is the gospel of grace. Having established a working understanding of what it means for Jesus Christ to be grace in his own person, we will then consider some suggestions with the Torrances on how the gospel of grace can be proclaimed in an "evangelical," as opposed to an "unevangelical," way.

This chapter is dedicated to those of us who are especially interested in the field of evangelism and are keen to proclaim a Christo-centric gospel to this and subsequent generations. As ambassadors for Christ, we can announce the accomplished fact that in Christ God has reconciled the world to himself, and instead of counting our trespasses against us,

---

1. Hereafter, in this chapter, designated TFT and JBT. While the two are of the same mind theologically, TFT has published a considerable amount more than his younger brother. This imbalance is reflected in the citations below.

5

has embraced humankind at enormous personal cost. This declaration of what God has done for the world, however, must never lose its performative element; that is, it is meant to evoke a response in people, so that they might believe the good news and live lives that reflect the truth of their reconciliation to God. As TFT reminds us, "at its heart evangelism is simply the attempt to persuade."[2] *Since, then, we know what it is to fear the Lord, we try to persuade men. . . . We implore you on Christ's behalf: Be reconciled to God* (2 Cor 5:11, 20).

Unfortunately, those attempting to persuade others of the truth of the gospel have often done so on unsound theological grounds and at times have even resorted to manipulative emotional and psychological tactics to produce "results." That is why *kerygma* and *didache* must be kept together. "In the language of the New Testament, preaching Christ . . . is both a *kerygmatic* and *didactic* activity. It is both evangelical and theological. . . . We need didactic preaching and kerygmatic theology."[3]

Theological persuasion, insist the Torrances, begins not with the "hows" and "whys" of evangelism but with the paramount theological question, "Who is Jesus Christ?" followed by "What has Christ accomplished in his person?" and finally "How can one participate in what has been accomplished in Christ?" All soteriological questions are therefore fundamentally christological ones; the work of Christ should never be detached from his person. The Torrances repeatedly cite John Calvin in this connection, for we must preach not a "naked Christ" but "Christ clothed with his gospel."[4]

As we shall see, the key to keeping together the person and work of Christ, his incarnation and atonement, is what the Torrances call the "vicarious humanity of Christ." Understanding the critical place of the vicarious humanity of Christ in theological persuasion entails an appreciation of ontology, or the nature of being. By becoming a human being, Christ bound up our being inextricably with his. When we discount this internal union that Christ established with each one of us via the incarnation, we empty the incarnation of soteriological significance and call men and women to respond from a center in themselves, external to Christ, instead of from *within* the incarnational union established by Christ in the Spirit. A loss of ontological perspective in evangelism has

2. TFT, *God and Rationality*, 206.

3. TFT, *Preaching Christ Today*, 1–2.

4. TFT, "Deposit of Faith," 19.

led to an undue amount of emphasis on the *acts* of Christ as apart from his *being*, and in turn to an emphasis on *acts* of subjective individual response apart from our *being* as linked with Christ's. This kind of "evangelism" that blurs the vicarious humanity of Christ "itself needs to be evangelized!" exclaims TFT.[5]

Viewed ontologically, the events of the gospel—incarnation, crucifixion, resurrection, ascension, and Pentecost—are held together in a deeply profound and trinitarian way. We begin to see that the gospel really is Jesus Christ, not just the benefits he procures for us. Our salvation is about participation by the Spirit in Christ's own being and in turn in the being of God. "Retrospectively, Christ came to save us from our past sin, from guilt, from judgment, from hell. But prospectively he came to bring us to sonship, to communion with God in the kingdom of God."[6] It is time in the evangelical community for us to consider the advantages of a grace-based evangelism that proclaims the adoption of all persons into the life of God and urges them to participate, by the Holy Spirit, in the relationship they have been given in Christ as the Father's sons and daughters.

> *But when the time had fully come, God sent his Son, born of a woman, born under the law, to redeem those under the law, that we might receive the full rights of sons. Because you are sons, God sent the Spirit of his Son into our hearts, the Spirit who calls out, "Abba, Father." So you are no longer a slave, but a son; and since you are a son, God has made you also an heir. (Gal 4:4–7)*

WHO IS JESUS CHRIST?

Creator and Redeemer

There is no better place to start in answer to the *who* question than Colossians chapter 1. Over and over the Torrances allude to its stunning portrayal of Jesus Christ, the Creator who became creature in order to re-create and redeem the universe from within our contingent existence: "Jesus IS Immanuel, Jesus IS God with us! Read the first chapter of St. Paul's Epistle to the Colossians; nothing is more breathtaking than what is written there—the Creator and Upholder of the whole universe of visible and invisible realities is identified with *Jesus*, and in him everything

---

5. TFT, *Preaching Christ Today*, 39.

6. JBT, *Worship, Community*, 62.

consists and is held together."[7] Whereas the world was created through Christ by virtue of "direct fiat," the redemption of the world was an "inside job," accomplished in the creaturely realm and in his person as a man "condescending to participate in finite being, submitting to its limitations and operating within its struggles and structures."[8]

God was pleased to have all God's fullness dwell "in the narrow constraint of a particular man."[9] Jesus was thus "the image of the invisible God" (Col 1:15), and as the *imago Dei* among us, redefines what the *imago Dei* is all about—not some "spark of the divine" inherent in humans, but humankind being created and uniquely adapted for a personal relationship with God.[10] In Christ God reveals the fact that "the *imago dei* is grounded in the divine will to create man in fellowship with himself" and manifests in his jealous love a stubborn refusal to let the contradiction of sin abrogate this original intention.[11]

> The Incarnation has to be thought of as the decisive intervention in our midst by the Love of God. . . . And so the whole miraculous fact of Jesus, his birth and life, his teaching and healing, his death and resurrection, is to be regarded as the chosen *locus* within our space and time where the order of redemption intersects and sublimates the order of creation so as to heal, enrich and advance it to a consummation in God's eternal purpose of Love beyond anything that we can conceive.[12]

In the marvelous symmetry of Colossians 1 we read that just as God created all things through Christ, all things are also reconciled to God through him, "making peace through his blood, shed on the cross" (Col 1:20). Of the cosmic significance of the cross of Christ, TFT comments:

> [The Atonement] has retroactive effect going back to the very beginning, and so Christ in the Apocalypse is spoken of as the First and the Last, the Alpha and the Omega. In the Cross we do not have mere amnesty for sin but such a total act of forgiveness and justification that guilt is utterly undone and done away. At the Cross God puts the clock back . . . and sets man's life on the basis of God's

7. TFT, *Preaching Christ Today*, 14.

8. TFT, *God and Rationality*, 144.

9. TFT, *Royal Priesthood*, 25.

10. TFT, *Christian Frame of Mind*, 31.

11. JBT, *Worship, Community*, 105, 103.

12. TFT, *Christian Frame of Mind*, 32.

creative purpose. *The Cross makes contact with creation.* Christ the Second, the Last Adam undoes the work of the First Adam and heads the race to a new and higher glory that far transcends the old, for here the past is not only undone but suborned by the Cross and made to serve the purpose of God's redemption.[13]

The resurrection was the validation of the efficacy of the life and cross of Christ, for instead of "succumbing to corruption in the grave and the disintegration of body and soul in death, Jesus rose again in the fulness and wholeness of his human being, thereby resurrecting human nature in himself."[14] Again with powerful symmetry Jesus is described in Colossians 1 as "the firstborn over all creation" *and* "the firstborn from among the dead" (Col 1:15, 18), denoting his birth as "proleptic to the resurrection of the dead, and building with it the birth of the new creation." To avoid divorcing the person and work of Christ we must remember that "*it is the whole Christ* . . . the Creator in our midst as human creature . . . *who is the content of the resurrection,* for all of his life from birth to resurrection forms an indissoluble unity."[15] As JBT adds, there is indeed a "duality-in-unity in the confession 'Jesus is Lord.' . . . He is Lord and Head as Creator and He is Lord and Head as the leader of our humanity."[16]

Throughout his earthly life, and not just in his death and resurrection, we see the Lord at work re-creating the world. That could hardly help but be the case considering the fact that even as creature Christ was still Creator, and it is borne out in his acts of mercy and healing—"the commanding fiat of the Creator was found on the lips of Jesus." Continues TFT: "In this union of the Creator with the creature the eternal Word of God who is the ground of man's existence from beyond his existence has now become also the ground of his existence within his

---

13. TFT, *Conflict and Agreement,* 1:255–56. Italics mine.

14. TFT, "Soul and Person," 107.

15. TFT, *Space, Time and Resurrection,* 60. Cf. 155: "Since he is the first-born of the new creation, the head in whom all things, visible and invisible, are reconciled and gathered up, the resurrection of Christ in *body* becomes the pledge that the whole physical universe will be renewed, for in a fundamental sense it has already been resurrected in Christ. It is understandable, therefore, that for classical Greek theology it was the resurrection, supervening upon the incarnation, that revealed the cosmic range of God's redeeming purpose."

16. JBT, "Vicarious Humanity and Priesthood," 70.

existence."[17] In the miracles of Jesus we see that he is already at work "reclaiming lost humanity, not by accusing men in their sickness and sin . . . , i.e. not by throwing the responsibility back upon them but by taking their responsibility on Himself."[18]

We must not let the divine activity of Christ cloud the fact that the Creator dwelt among us not *in* a man but *as* man. The astounding import of this for all of us is spelled out by TFT:

> He who was made flesh is the Creator Logos by whom all things were made and in whom all things are upheld. When he became incarnate, and divine and human natures were united in his one person, his humanity was brought into an ontological relation with all creation. So far as our humanity is concerned that means that all men are upheld, whether they know it or not, in their humanity by Jesus Christ the true and proper man, upheld by the fulfilment and establishment of true humanity in him, but also through his work in the cross and resurrection in which he overcame the degenerating forces of evil and raised up our human nature out of death and perdition.[19]

The evangelistic implications of Jesus Christ as Creator and Redeemer as expounded in Colossians 1 must not be missed. By virtue of the incarnation, our being has been gathered up into his, the one in whom "all things hold together" (Col 1:17). "If it is in God, then it is in God incarnate in Jesus, that all human beings live and move and have their being,"[20] or, to say it another way, "the secret of every man, whether he believes it or not, is bound up with Jesus."[21]

A Covenant God, Not a Contract God

As we have seen, the incarnation reveals that Jesus Christ is one with us and one with God. "In Christ all the fullness of the Deity lives in bodily form" (Col 2:9); he is "the visible expression of the invisible God" (Col 1:15 JBP), and thus we *really* can say that to see Jesus is to see God the Father Almighty, Maker of heaven and earth. In Jesus' own words: *Anyone who has seen me has seen the Father. How can you say, "Show us*

---

17. TFT, *God and Rationality*, 143–44.
18. TFT, "Service in Jesus Christ," 5.
19. TFT, *Space, Time and Resurrection*, 154–55.
20. TFT, "Atonement," 230–31.
21. TFT, *Trinitarian Faith*, 183.

the Father"? (John 14:9). Adhering to the theological dictum that what God is toward us he is in his innermost being, the Torrances are certain that to try to construct a doctrine of God controlled by anything other than God's self-revelation in Christ is to leave a "realist foundation" and to stand on dangerous hermeneutical footing.[22] Unfortunately, our theological approach has often been backward, fitting Jesus Christ into a preconceived doctrine of God.[23]

What is needed, urge the Torrances, is a disciplined approach to theology that is not unlike scientific study, where the investigation is governed by the nature of the subject matter itself and not by more indirect notions. In the case of "scientific theology," then, we must always strive to interpret God out of God, cognizant that God has been revealed most directly and completely in the person of Jesus Christ, he in whom "all the fullness of the Deity lives in bodily form" (Col 2:9). The Torrances will never let us stray from the critical orthodox doctrine of the *homoousion*, which insists against all forms of Arianism that Jesus Christ is not "of like being" with the Father but "of one being" with the Father.[24]

Could it be that God wants all of our God-talk to be controlled by the incarnation? The alternative "means that even Christian forms of

22. TFT interview, "Pilgrimage," 63. Cf. 61, where TFT expresses a desire to write commentaries on Colossians and Hebrews: "My intention in these volumes is really, quite frankly, to collapse modern biblical interpretation from behind—for I think it is basically wrong—and to try to build up a much more firm basis for a realist hermeneutic in which God's self-revelation can come through to us on its own ground and in its own integrity."

23. JBT, "Doctrine of the Trinity," 12–13. From his own experience JBT critiques the traditional approach to teaching theology: "No Christian doctrine was taught in the first year—only the philosophy of religion. This meant that the student *began* by considering (a) the possibility of belief in God—arguments for his existence (Aquinas' 'five ways,' etc.); grounds for disbelief (problem of evil); the concept of miracles in the scientific age, etc., (b) the nature of religious language, the possibility of 'God-talk': verification and falsification, etc. Once there had been established (outside of revelation) some kind of rationale for believing in God, only then, in the second year, were the doctrines of the Incarnation and Trinity taught, as though to be *grafted on to* a previous conception of God."

24. JBT, "Interpreting the Word," 257. TFT adds on the *homoousion*: "The kingpin of the Nicene-Constantinopolitan Creed was the *homoousion*—the affirmation of oneness in being between the Son—and indeed the incarnate Son—and the Father. Without that ontic unity there is no Mediator between God and man and the identity of Jesus Christ has nothing to do with any self-giving or self-revealing on the part of the eternal God, in which event the whole structure not only of the Creed but of the Gospel itself would disintegrate and collapse" (TFT, *Incarnation*, xi).

thought and speech about God are uprooted from any objective ground in the being of God himself and float loose in the vague mists of modern man's vaunted self-understanding."[25] Everything depends on trusting the picture of God we get in Jesus, while determining to avoid our own mythological projections.[26]

> It is only through this encounter with Jesus Christ in His implacable objectivity in which we become crucified to the world and to ourselves that we are enabled to know objectively as we are known by Him and so to think appropriately of God in accordance with his nature, and not out of a centre in ourselves in which we impose our own patterns of thought upon Him and then fail to distinguish Him in His reality from our own subjective states and conditions. It is only in and through Jesus Christ that man's eclipse of God can come to an end.[27]

What do we discover when we begin to develop a doctrine of God through the incarnation and atonement instead of the other way around? We see Jesus Christ as "the Word and Hand of God stretched out to save us, the very heart of God Almighty beating with the pulse of his infinite love."[28] We discover an inner consistency in the God who loved the world so much that he gave his only begotten Son to die for sinners. "What God is in his Being (Father, Son and Holy Spirit) he is in all his acts, and what he is in his acts, he is eternally and antecedently in his Being—Holy Love."[29] We do not need to look behind Jesus for some God behind God, some "dark inscrutable God" or "arbitrary Deity."[30]

"God is love," emphasizes JBT, and "love always implies a communion between persons. . . . The Father loves the Son in the communion of the Spirit. The Son loves the Father in the communion of the Spirit. God has his being in communion."[31] Elsewhere he adds: "Who is the God who created Adam? He is the triune God whose nature is love, and who is in creation . . . what he is in his innermost being, the God who reveals

---

25. TFT, "Church," 754.

26. TFT, *Ground and Grammar*, 40.

27. TFT, "Eclipse of God," 213.

28. TFT, *Incarnation*, xv.

29. JBT, "Strengths and Weaknesses of Westminster," 50–51.

30. TFT, *Incarnation*, xvi–xvii.

31. JBT, *Worship, Community*, 61.

himself in covenant love in Christ, and who brings [to] fulfilment in redemption his purposes in creation."[32]

"What our doctrine of God is, that is our anthropology." If we interpret creation christologically we begin to see that from the beginning God's prime purpose for humans is a filial one, to be children of the Heavenly Father and folded into the trinitarian relations.[33] Again quoting TFT:

> The astonishing revelation of God in the Biblical Tradition is that God does not wish to exist alone, and has freely brought into being alongside of himself and yet in utter distinction from himself another upon whom he may pour out his love, with whom he may share his divine Life in covenant-partnership. That is the relationship in terms of which the ultimate secret of human nature is to be sought. . . . What greater dignity could man have?[34]

We have been talking about the dignity of humanity being secured as God's covenant partner and the object of his affection. But what exactly do we mean by "covenant" in this context? "Theologically speaking, a covenant is a promise binding two people or two parties to love one another unconditionally," says JBT. Alternatively, a contract is "a legal relationship in which two people or parties bind themselves together on mutual conditions to effect some future result. . . . It takes the form, 'If . . . if . . . then . . . ,' as in the business world. . . . God's dealings with men in Creation and in Redemption—in grace—are those of Covenant and not of contract."[35] Again, by "looking through" the oneness of the Creator-Redeemer we can see that God's covenant of grace extends back past Israel to Adam, and that "the covenant relationship between God and Israel . . . was a particularization of the one covenant of grace which embraced the whole of creation."[36]

The amazing thing about God's covenant of grace with humanity and with Israel is that, unlike a bilateral covenant, it is not contingent upon the mutual response of both parties:[37]

32. JBT, "Incarnation and Limited Atonement," 92–93.

33. JBT, "Concept of Federal Theology," 35.

34. TFT, "Goodness and Dignity," 314.

35. JBT, "Covenant or Contract," 54.

36. TFT, *God and Rationality*, 146.

37. JBT, "Covenant or Contract," 55. See, regarding God's covenant of grace with Israel, TFT: "The covenant between God and Israel was not a covenant between God

> While the covenant relationship was disclosed through its con-
> crete realisation in God's relations with historic Israel, it has been
> *unilaterally* set up by God between himself and all mankind, to
> which he remains everlastingly faithful and which he *unilaterally*
> upholds no matter whether the covenant partner fulfils his part
> in the relationship or not. God can no more break his covenant of
> Love and Truth with mankind than he can cease to be God.[38]

Yet despite its unilateral character, inherent in God's covenant promise "I shall be your God and you shall be my people" is the call for a response—"a response of faith and gratitude and love."[39] "God in grace, in covenant love, creates Adam for covenant love and then lays him under unconditional obligations, warning him of the consequences which would follow 'if' he transgresses these commandments." This "if" is, according to JBT, "what we might call a 'descriptive IF' (a description of the consequences which would follow disobedience) not a 'prescriptive IF' (a prescription of the conditions which under grace can be obtained)."[40] In other words, the obligations of grace must never be misconstrued into the conditions of grace. God's promised love is pure and unconditional. In fact, "there is no such thing as conditional love." To say "I love you IF . . ." is to say "I don't love you."[41]

Unfortunately, the biblical concept of covenant has been corrupted by the introduction of the so-called covenant of works, which first appeared in theological discourse at the end of the sixteenth century, and which, while never taught by Calvin himself, was adopted enthusiastically by the Calvinist movement. For Calvin, there was "one eternal Covenant of Grace promised in the Old Testament and fulfilled in

---

and a holy people, but precisely the reverse. It was a covenant established out of pure grace between God and Israel in its sinful, rebellious and estranged existence. Hence, no matter how rebellious or sinful Israel was, it could not escape the love and faithfulness of God" (TFT, *Mediation of Christ*, 27–28).

38. TFT, *Christian Theology*, 82. Italics mine.

39. JBT, "Covenant or Contract," 55. God has never put humans under conditions of grace. "It is false to interpret OT worship as legalistic and only New Testament worship as the way of grace. . . . The sacrifice of lambs and bulls and goats were not ways of placating an angry God, currying favor with God as in the pagan worship of the Baalim. They were God-given covenantal witnesses to grace—that the God who alone could wipe out their sins would be gracious. God is always the subject of propitiation, never its object" (JBT, *Worship, Community*, 50).

40. JBT, "Incarnation and Limited Atonement," 90, 90n.

41. JBT, "Covenant Concept," 228.

Christ. 'Old' and 'New' do not mean two covenants, but two forms of the one eternal covenant."[42] Adversely, Calvinists made the covenant of law primary for all, and grace followed as the exception for the "elect." By doing so, they "substituted a legal understanding of man for a filial one," says JBT, but "this yields an impersonal view of man, as the object of justice, rather than the object of love. . . . In the New Testament, God's prime purpose in Creation, Incarnation, Atonement, and the gift of the Spirit at Pentecost is filial, not just legal—'to bring sons to glory.'"[43]

Surely JBT is right when he declares that "the sin of the human heart in all ages . . . [is] to try to turn God's covenant of grace into a contract."[44] His brother adds: "Through deeply ingrained habits (that is, by virtue of original sin) we want in some measure to deserve or earn the Grace of God. . . . Thus we tend regularly to interpret God's unilateral covenant mercies within a frame of thought such as the so-called 'covenant of works' invented by Calvinists, in which the self-giving of God in undiluted Grace is held after all to be conditional on our human responses."[45]

Covenant, not contract; grace over law; filial over judicial—these emphases help us to keep in mind that "the Bible is Good News from beginning to end."[46] When these truths become skewed, however, the damage done in evangelism is considerable, for we make forgiveness conditional on repentance and "we hesitate in the name of Christ to proclaim absolution and free forgiveness of sins, or hesitate to believe that we are truly forgiven."[47] These implications for evangelism we shall discuss further. For now let it suffice to say that JBT's declaration "The God of the Bible is a covenant God, not a contract God"[48] must stay at the forefront of our thinking regarding theological persuasion.

We certainly think of Jesus Christ as Lord and Redeemer, but perhaps we are less likely to think of him as Creator. Perhaps we are less likely to think of him as the covenant God of Abraham, Isaac, and Jacob. Yet this is exactly what we need to do if we are to have a full-orbed answer to the *who* question. If we do not interpret creation and covenant

42. TFT, *Mediation of Christ*, 299.

43. JBT, "Interpreting the Word," 265.

44. JBT, "Covenant or Contract," 56.

45. TFT, *Christian Theology*, 82–83.

46. JBT, "Vicarious Humanity and Priesthood," 79.

47. JBT, "Covenant or Contract," 66.

48. JBT, "Concept of Federal Theology," 37.

christologically, we will have a false doctrine of God, a false doctrine of humanity, and an inability to rightly assess sin and law. This can only cause a theological train wreck in our proclamation ministry.

For example, while the Father sent his only begotten Son into the world, we must also preach the incarnation as a *self*-giving of God to the world. In other words, it should become clear that God (Father, Son, and Holy Spirit) has always had a merciful, loving attitude toward humanity, and that the incarnation does not signify a shift in God's attitude toward us but is an extravagant outpouring on behalf of his beloved. To say anything else is to introduce a false split within God, as if the Father and the Son were not of one heart on the matter of how to save the world. This leads to egregious concepts of the Son having to appease the Father on our behalf, or of our need to "plead the blood" of Christ for God to tolerate us. On the contrary, God simply refused to let his filial purposes be thwarted by sin, and he resolved to deal with humanity's corruption thoroughly and completely in his Son.

Concerning the law, if we preach that God defines us first and foremost in legal terms, making justice the fundamental attribute of God, then God's love can only be arbitrary. In this view, it cannot be said that God loves everyone. God is not holy love in his innermost being. God's grace and love are lavished only on those who prove their election by their repentance. Instead of beginning with grace, then, evangelism in this view begins with what the Puritans called "law-work," using the law as a schoolmaster to lead lost souls to Christ.[49] If people do repent in this context, will their view of God be a healthy one? Will they be confident of God's gracious attitude toward them?

Who is Jesus Christ? "The doctrine of the incarnation is that he is at once the God who gives us the two tables of the law, who commands us to love our enemies, and he is the one who as man for us fulfilled the law—loving his enemies, praying for those who despitefully used him and rejected him. Does God tell us to love all men, including our enemies, but he himself does not?"[50] Those who answer in the affirmative can only produce a cockeyed doctrine of God that fails to allow all thought of God to be controlled by the incarnation of Jesus Christ, "the radiance of God's glory and the exact representation of his being" (Heb 1:3).

49. JBT, "Strengths and Weaknesses of Westminster," 49. I would argue that this "law-work" approach misreads Galatians 3:24.

50. JBT, "Incarnation and Limited Atonement," 86.

As we have seen, true knowledge of God does not come *a priori*, but only *a posteriori*, as derived from the revelation of Jesus Christ. He is the way, the truth, and the life, and there is no way to cut behind Jesus to get to God.[51] "Now that the Incarnation has taken place we must think of it as the decisive action of God in Christ which invalidates all other possibilities and makes all other conceivable roads within space and time to God actually unthinkable."[52] There is at once the most profound exclusivity and inclusivity related to Christ; he is the unique mediator whose mediation embraced all men. "To preach Christ to men, women, and children today we must proclaim him in his uncompromising singularity and transcendence as the one Lord and Savior of the world."[53]

We are now prepared to consider more deeply the soteriological significance of the mediator Jesus Christ, he who was just as fully and truly human as he was fully and truly God.

THE SOTERIOLOGICAL INVERSION IN THE PERSON OF JESUS CHRIST

Mediator

As an entry point for our discussion of the mediation of Christ, let us return to the doctrine of the covenant of grace established for Adam and his descendants. We saw that the law has its proper place in the context of grace; "law is the gift of grace" and "spells out the obligations of grace."[54] JBT adds elsewhere: "There are no limits to God's grace, there are no conditions to God's grace, but He calls us to a life of unconditional faith and love and obedience in every area of life."[55] Yet while we may appreciate the unconditional nature of God's unilateral covenant with us, the question that begs to be answered is, How are we to respond? These obligations of grace are too lofty for us; they feel burdensome. If God gave us a law God knew we could not keep, can it really be said that the law is a gift of grace?

---

51. TFT, *Space, Time and Resurrection*, 134.

52. TFT, *Space, Time and Incarnation*, 68.

53. TFT, *Preaching Christ Today*, 27. See also 25, where TFT critiques the "multi-faith" approach of missionaries who present Christianity "as one religion in a universal class of religions."

54. JBT, "Strengths and Weaknesses of Westminster," 49.

55. JBT, "Covenant or Contract," 240.

To these questions we find the answer in the mediator Jesus Christ, for the obligations of "unconditional faith and love and obedience" we are called to in the covenant of grace are fulfilled by him on our behalf. The wonderful truth of the gospel is that Jesus Christ "fulfilled the covenant from both sides: 'I will be your God, and you will be my people.' 'I am holy, be you holy.' 'I will be your Father and you will be my son.'"[56] This does not mean that Jesus kept a covenant of *works* on our behalf; that would be to misinterpret the function of the law and to de-emphasize the covenant of *grace* that preceded Sinai and gave the Torah its inner meaning (cf. Gal 3:17).

Christ's mediation takes us far past abject obedience to the law by restoring to us our filial relationship with God.

> What we are concerned with is the filial relation which the Son of God lived out in our humanity in perfect holiness and love, achieving that in himself in assuming our human nature into oneness with himself, and on that ground giving us to share in it, providing us with a fulness in his own obedient Sonship from which we may all receive.[57]

Jesus Christ is our representative and substitute "in all our relations with God, including every aspect of human response to Him: such as trusting and obeying, understanding and knowing, loving and worshipping." This divinely provided response we have in Christ on our behalf and in our place is what is known as "the all-significant middle term, . . . the vicarious humanity of Christ."[58]

The mediation of Christ must not be thought of as a normal human mediation—the stepping in of a third party to mediate between two others. Nor must Christ's substitution for us in life and death be thought of instrumentally, as if somehow his righteousness and filial obedience were imputed to us in an external way. The doctrine of "substitutionary atonement" is often explained in this manner, and the term "vicarious" is in turn attached only to the death of Christ. The vicarious *humanity* of Christ defines the atonement not instrumentally but ontologically, for Christ "was one and the same being as God and one and the same being

---

56. TFT, *Mediation of Christ*, 77.

57. TFT, *Theology in Reconstruction*, 156.

58. TFT, *God and Rationality*, 145. See *Mediation of Christ* on the necessity of keeping "representative" and "substitute" together in our thinking of the vicarious humanity of Christ.

as man. His mediation took place, therefore, both within his ontological relations with God and within his ontological relations with mankind."[59] TFT elaborates:

> We are to think of the whole life and activity of Jesus from the cradle to the grave as constituting the vicarious human response to himself which God has freely and unconditionally provided for us. . . . Jesus Christ *is* our human response to God. . . . If Jesus is a substitute in detachment from us, who simply acts in our stead in an external, formal or forensic way, then his response has no ontological bearing upon us but is an empty transaction over our heads.[60]

In a "double movement of grace," Jesus Christ has represented God to us and us to God. Therefore, we can say with JBT: "In the deepest sense Jesus Christ is himself the atonement."[61] Because he is fully God and fully man in one person (the hypostatic union), he has accomplished at-one-ment, uniting humanity with himself. "The coming of the Son of God into our lost and alienated being constitutes *Immanuel*, God with us, but if God is with us in Christ then in him we are with God. *We with God* is thus the obverse of *God with us*,"[62] adds TFT. This is what Calvin and the church fathers called the wonderful exchange: The Son of God became Son of Man so that we, sons of men, might become sons of God.

Drawing on the patristic emphases of Irenaeus, Athanasius, Cyril of Alexandria, and the Cappadocians, the Torrances are endeavoring to bring the church back to a deeper appreciation for the incarnation. They are certain that going to the Scriptures with preconceived notions of external relations regarding the atonement has clouded the truth about atonement taking place "within the incarnate being of the Son of God and in his ontological solidarity with mankind."[63] For the Greek fathers, "the incarnation was seen to be essentially redemptive and redemption was seen to be inherently incarnational or ontological."[64]

All of this talk of incarnational/ontological atonement is enough to make most of us Westerners squirm in our seats! Does not an emphasis

59. TFT, "Atonement," 235.

60. TFT, *Mediation of Christ*, 80.

61. JBT, *Worship, Community*, 204.

62. TFT, *Space, Time and Resurrection*, 47.

63. TFT, *Trinitarian Faith*, 157.

64. Ibid., 159.

here belie a diluting of the significance of the cross? On the contrary, the Torrances are keen to show that a primary emphasis on the ontological can only lead to a greater and deeper appreciation for the expiatory and propitiatory elements of the atonement.

> In Western Christianity the atonement tends to be interpreted almost exclusively in terms of forensic relations as a judicial trans-action in the transference of the penalty for sin from the sinner to the sin-bearer. In the biblical and early patristic tradition, however, as we have seen, the Incarnation and the atonement are internally linked, for atoning expiation and propitiation are worked out in the ontological depths of human being and existence into which the Son of God penetrated as the Son of Mary.[65]

Indeed, if we lose the ontological aspect of redemption, it is our the-ology of the cross that is most adversely affected. As an external transac-tion, Christ's death can be the cost for sin without actually touching *us!* The pardoning of a criminal may affect the criminal (as in an Abelardian view of the atonement), but it does not necessarily or effectually change the criminal; in the same way, the ransom paid by Christ loses its valid-ity if he is not already united to us. The biblical testimony is that when Christ died, we all died with him (2 Cor 5:14).

God determined that victory would not be won from the outside, even if only one step removed, as if our righteousness were imputed to us like some legal fiction. Incarnational union and imputation must cleave together. The doctor does not just give us medicine; "he becomes the patient!" exclaims JBT, and "our humanity is healed in him, in his person. We are not just healed through Christ, because of the work of Christ, but in and through Christ."[66] Any attempts at self-restoration by sinful creatures end in futility, adds TFT, for "all they do partakes of what they are . . . , so God himself became a creature in order to do for the creature what the creature could in no way do for itself."[67]

If ignoring the incarnational union damages our theology of the cross, it also can blind us to the seriousness of sin. The Torrances again adhere to the premise of the Greek fathers, that "the unassumed is the unhealed." If we have Jesus only in semisolidarity with us, as if taking on some kind of neutral human nature, then we will certainly be less able to

65. TFT, *Mediation of Christ*, 40.

66. JBT, *Worship, Community*, 42–43.

67. TFT, *Divine and Contingent Order*, 135.

appreciate the lifelong sacrifice he made, or the depths he plumbed, to undo our evil from the very roots. The Torrances never tire of expressing the extent of Christ's solidarity with fallen humanity, and that "it was not only our actual sins, but it was original sin and original guilt that the Son of God took upon himself."[68]

> Thus Athanasius could say that "the whole Christ became a curse for us," for in taking upon himself the form of a servant, the Lord transferred to himself fallen Adamic humanity which he took from the Virgin Mary, that is, our perverted, corrupt, degenerate, diseased human nature enslaved to sin and subject to death under the condemnation of God. However, far from sinning himself or being contaminated by what he appropriated from us, Christ triumphed over the forces of evil entrenched in our human existence, bringing his own holiness, his own perfect obedience, to bear upon it in such a way as to condemn sin in the flesh and deliver us from its power [Rom 8:3; 2 Cor 5:21].[69]

By not specifically mentioning the cross above, TFT is promoting a broader view of the work of Christ. As we have seen, the Torrances firmly believe with the Fathers that "the incarnation is itself redemptive and not just a means to an end."[70] With Calvin they insist that Christ's redemptive work began at the initiation of the hypostatic union, when Christ was conceived by the Holy Spirit and became man. At the same time, they acknowledge that the "centre and heart of that incredible movement of God's love is located in the cross of Christ."[71] It was here, where Christ put himself under the utmost wickedness, that the internal relations so necessary to our salvation most threatened to crumble. TFT comments on this unfathomable pressure put upon the hypostatic union in the person of Christ, and the result:

> That was a living and dynamic union which ran throughout the whole of his life, in which he maintained union and communion with the Father in the steadfastness of the Father toward the Son and in the steadfastness of the Son toward the Father. The resur-

---

68. TFT, "Reconciliation of Mind," 199.

69. TFT, *Trinitarian Faith*, 161. In "Reconciliation of Mind," 199, TFT notes a fragment from Irenaeus, no doubt known to Athanasius, that relates incarnational atonement to the story of Jesus and the leper. For Jesus did not shrink back from touching the leper, but upon doing so he healed the "sinner" instead of becoming leprous himself.

70. TFT, *Preaching Christ Today*, 59.

71. TFT, *Divine and Contingent Order*, 138.

> rection means that this union did not give way but held under the strain imposed not only by the forces that sought to divide Jesus from God, but the strain imposed through the infliction of the righteous judgment of the Father upon our rebellious humanity which Christ had made his own—and it held under the strain imposed by both in the crucifixion: the hypostatic union survived the descent into hell and Christ arose still in unbroken communion with the Father.[72]

When Christ rose from the dead, we all rose with him; the birth of the new humanity was complete.

Our Brother and Great High Priest

In all this talk about incarnation and atonement, we must not lose sight of God's loving motive to restore and reconstitute his filial relationship with us, that the Son Jesus Christ might be "the firstborn among many brothers" (Rom 8:29).

> In Jesus Christ the Son of the Father has personally entered into our human existence where we have forfeited our rights as children of God, interpenetrated the structures of our personal and interpersonal being-constituting relations as sons and daughters in the creaturely family of God which we have polluted and falsified, twisting them round into their opposite so that instead of expressing genuine filial relation to the heavenly Father they express what we are in our self-centered alienation from him and from one another, thus turning the truth of the very image of God into a lie. But having entered and made his own that estranged and disobedient condition of our human being, he has converted it back in his own human being in love and obedience to the Father.[73]

We have been converted in Christ! While this is not normally how we think of the term "conversion," yet it is nonetheless true and we must begin to think this way if we are to take our ontological union with Jesus Christ seriously. When Karl Barth, who mentored the Torrances, was asked, "When were you converted?" he gave the unexpected answer: "I was converted nineteen hundred years ago when Jesus Christ died for

---

72. TFT, *Space, Time and Resurrection*, 54.
73. TFT, *Mediation of Christ*, 79.

my sins and rose again."[74] In like manner, JBT presents a twofold elaboration on Christ's solidarity with us:

> [1.] When Jesus was born for us at Bethlehem, was baptized by the Spirit in the Jordan, suffered under Pontius Pilate, rose again and ascended, our humanity was born again, baptized by the Spirit, suffered, died, rose again and ascended in him, in his representative vicarious humanity. *Now he presents us in himself* to the Father as God's dear children, and our righteousness is hid with Christ in God, ready to be revealed at the last day.

> [2.] Conversely, because Jesus has lived our life, offered himself through the eternal Spirit without spot to the Father in our name and on our behalf, as the one for the many, *God accepts us in him.* We are accepted in the beloved Son—immaculate in him, and only in him—"holy and blameless in his sight" (Eph 1:4).[75]

These two statements, anchored by the phrases *he presents us in himself* and *God accepts us in him,* are based on Christ's high priestly ministry modeled after that in the Old Testament:

> In the worship of old Israel, the high priest represented God to Israel and Israel to God in his own person. The Covenant between God and Israel was concentrated as it were in the person of the high priest. It is this thought which lies behind the New Testament and patristic understanding of the inclusive and representative humanity of Christ, the Mediator of the New Covenant, who represents God to man and man to God in His own Person, as the One on behalf of the Many.[76]

---

74. JBT, *Worship, Community,* 64.

75. Ibid., 39. Italics mine. Interestingly, JBT presents at least two other versions of this twofold statement in his writings. Cf. "Priesthood of Jesus," 170; "Vicarious Humanity and Priesthood," 76. The one cited here is the only one I noticed that substitutes "our humanity was born again" for "we were born again." Possibly this is an attempt to de-emphasize the objective nature of our personal rebirth and to include the subjective pole. If that is correct, it would be unusual, since the Torrances are normally intent on emphasizing the oft-overlooked ontological, or objective, pole. Cf. "Strengths and Weaknesses of Westminster," 44, where JBT critiques the *Shorter Catechism* for not considering the vicarious humanity in a section on sanctification: "It is well stated, but the concern is entirely with sanctification *in us,* i.e. sanctification subjectively considered, with not a word about Christ as the one who assumed our humanity and sanctified it *for us* by His life in the Spirit." Later in the study we will discuss the objective-subjective issue at length.

76. JBT, "Vicarious Humanity and Priesthood," 74.

The ongoing and once-for-all high priestly ministry of Jesus Christ in Hebrews is a treasure chest regarding the vicarious humanity of Christ, and begs for more attention than we can give it here. No other book of the Bible has a richer combination of references to both Christ's deity (see 1:1–4) and his humanity (see 2:9–18). As John Calvin and the Greek fathers both realized, the high priestly role combines the representative and sacrificial elements of atonement in a unique and powerful way; Jesus is the "One for the many," priest *and* victim.[77]

Because they have direct bearing on our study regarding evangelical persuasion, we must pause to consider a couple of potentially confusing features of JBT's twofold statement above. First, his apparent parallel of Jesus' birth in Bethlehem and our rebirth. As we have seen, the Torrances would want to present the redemptive life of Christ as a unified whole; the birth, life, death, and resurrection of Christ taken together *is* the re-creation of humanity.[78] With this is an understanding that Christ's resurrection is proleptic to his birth, because it is *Christ's* resurrection and *Christ's* birth; the Christ-event includes all of the historical events of Christ. One's own existential moment of rebirth, by the Holy Spirit, is very real. But it is real precisely because this "Joe-event" or "Jane-event" is rooted in the eternal reality of the Christ-event, where Christ acted and continues to act on Joe and Jane's behalf. These historical events of the gospel, seen within the unified whole, do not only build on one another chronologically or sequentially; they also interpenetrate one another. That's why we can say that Christ's resurrection and birth are proleptic to one another, and also that our own particular and contemporary rebirth, many years later, is actually contained in these events.

77. Ibid., 73. One of the greatest theological influences on the Torrances is John McLeod Campbell. With Campbell, they assert that even the confession of our sins is mediated by Christ, the perfect penitent. While not a sinner himself, Jesus said in his flesh the perfect "Amen" to the just judgment of God.

78. The glaring omission from this list is Pentecost, which will soon be given its due! It is only the Holy Spirit who brings the reality of the gospel to bear in existential and contemporary situations. That is why the word *proleptic*, meaning without consideration of chronology, is especially useful. This is not meant in any way to dehistoricize the gospel events but to give full force to the eternal nature of Jesus Christ. This allows us, for instance, to hypostatically view the cross as a saving event in itself, even before the resurrection, because it is Jesus Christ, the one who said "I AM the resurrection," who was crucified. Likewise, by the Holy Spirit we can confidently say that we actually died in Christ, even before we died, and that even now we are seated at the right hand of the Father in the heavenly realms.

But we must go even further. There is also a sense in which *each* of the gospel components listed above contains the re-creation of humanity in itself. So our re-creation is contained not only in Christ's birth, death, and resurrection bundled together, even proleptically, but also separately. Altogether then, and in a fashion not dissimilar to the unity and particularity intrinsic to trinitarian relations, we can know that each gospel event is a part, each is the whole, and together they are the whole. Thus equipped, we are prepared to better understand the different ways of describing our regeneration as put forth by TFT:

> Our regeneration has already taken place and is fully enclosed in the birth and resurrection of Christ, and proceeds from them more by way of manifestation of what has already happened than as a new effect resulting from them.[79]

> When were you born again? In your conversion? In your Baptism? The profoundest answer you can give to that question is, when Jesus Christ was born from above by the Holy Spirit. The birth of Jesus was the birth of the new man, and it is in Him and through sharing in his birth that we are born again.[80]

Concerning the famous passage in John chapter 3, TFT asserts: "That is the point also of Jesus' conversation with Nicodemus, that our birth of water and of the Spirit is not a carnal but a spiritual event, from above, and behind it lies the primary reality of Christ's birth, for it is He who is the One born from above, who descended from heaven."[81]

In *The Mediation of Christ*, TFT resorts to stronger language to get his critical point across:

> It is significant that the New Testament does not use the term regeneration (*paliggenesia*), as so often modern evangelical theology does, for what goes on in the human heart. . . . We must speak of Jesus Christ as constituting the very substance of our

79. TFT, *Conflict and Agreement*, 2:131.

80. Ibid., 128.

81. Ibid., 118. TFT also cites examples in 1 John 5:18, where "born of God" refers primarily to Jesus and only secondarily to the believer: "The Christian's birth described in the perfect tense is rather the result that accrues from that [primary event] rather than an event in itself; it is the effect or fruit of that unique event, and is not something in addition to it, but a sharing in it"; and John 1:12, 13: "All the patristic citations of this verse in the second and early part of the third centuries (Irenaeus, Tertullian, Hippolytus, etc.) cite it in the singular with direct reference to the virgin birth of Christ. . . . We are born again in Christ's miraculous birth."

conversion, so that we must think of him as taking our place even in our acts of repentance and personal decision, for without him all so-called repentance and conversion are empty. Since a conversion in that truly evangelical sense is a turning away from ourselves to Christ, it calls for *a conversion from our inward notions of conversion* to one which is grounded and sustained in Christ Jesus himself.[82]

The last sentence above could be the summary statement for this entire study, and we shall delve into its implications.

Our second concern is with JBT's appearing to present Ephesians 1:4 ("For he chose us in him before the creation of the world to be holy and blameless in his sight") as universally applicable via the incarnational union established by Christ with humanity. Let us begin here with a few preliminary remarks. Undoubtedly, Scripture is wonderfully ambiguous in places, and because the Epistles are addressed to Christians, it is a challenge to look "through" the letters for universal truths (Calvin spoke of the Holy Scripture as spectacles in this way).[83] Yet if the truth of Christ is the only truth there is, there is no reason why biblical interpreters cannot mine through the letters written to Christians, peeling off the layers regarding their belief in the truth, to glimpse the core truth itself.

This process fundamentally concerns the point of view the interpreter brings to the text. No one comes to the Bible from a point of neutrality; everyone brings his or her own theological presuppositions. Instead of denying this fact, we should acknowledge it. We should then hold our preconceived notions "loosely," testing them as we immerse ourselves in the texts and humbly and prayerfully look for the trajectory that is most solidly substantiated by the Word.

If we read Scripture with the Torrances—that is, in a manner controlled by the *who* question and aligned with "the living word" (1 Pet 1:23)—Scripture begins to unfold in new and exciting ways for us. Concepts such as ontological solidarity, incarnational union, and the vicarious humanity of Christ begin to emerge with clarity. The "Torrancian" trajectory is not new itself, however; on the contrary, this is an exegetical line taken by many of the giants of the early church (e.g., Irenaeus, Athanasius, Cyril, Basil, Gregory of Nazianzus). For the Fathers, notes TFT,

---

82. TFT, *Mediation of Christ*, 85–86. Italics mine.

83. TFT, "Pilgrimage," 64.

the *homoousion* took on the role of an interpretive frame through which general understanding of the evangelical and apostolic witness was given more exact guidance throughout the Church. What the *homoousion* did was to give expression to the ontological substructure upon which the meaning of various biblical texts rested and through which they were integrated.[84]

Now concerning JBT's interpretation of Ephesians 1:4: "For he chose us in him before the creation of the world to be holy and blameless in his sight." If we begin by asking, "Who is Jesus Christ?" we may, through the *homoousion*, establish the premise that Jesus Christ is one with the being of God, and that, because all human being exists in the being of God, there is an internal link between Jesus Christ and all of humanity. That is in fact what Paul goes on to say in Ephesians 1:10. Because Jesus Christ is the representative Head of every human being, inherent in the statement of verse 4 is the understanding that all humanity's reconciliation, justification, and sanctification has been accomplished in Christ. He is "our righteousness, holiness, and redemption" (1 Cor 1:30), for example, not because he became this when we believed, but simply because he *is*. "He is the One in whose death we died, in whose body we were raised, and in whose continuing humanity our humanity is presented by our Great High Priest to the Father."[85]

In light of his solidarity with us as high priest, we can apprehend the concept that when Christ assumed our corrupt flesh, he sanctified it through his life of uncompromising filial obedience. He thereby "brothered" us, fulfilling the covenant of grace as he was faithful and true to himself on our behalf. Surely this is the meaning of the high priestly prayer, "For their sakes I sanctify myself, that they also may be sanctified by the truth" (John 17:19), and the words in Hebrews, "For both he that sanctifieth and they who are sanctified are all of one, for He is not ashamed to call them brethren" (Heb 2:11).[86]

At this stage of our study questions emerge concerning evangelism. After all, isn't this idea of solidarity too inclusive and the part about everyone being "born again" in Christ a bit extreme? If everything is accomplished by Christ on our behalf already, does this not undermine the whole concept of evangelism? Is there not a place for our own personal response to the gospel? Where is the leverage to convince people

84. TFT, *Incarnation*, xii.

85. JBT, "Place of Christ in Worship," 357.

86. JBT, "Vicarious Humanity and Priesthood," 75.

of their need for deliverance—isn't this soft on sin? Isn't this universalism? These are healthy questions, and it is not surprising that Western rugged individualists tend to bristle when faced with the objective truth of what has happened *to* them in Christ! We will address these questions in due course, but we have not even yet considered the full picture of the salvation that has been wrought for us by the Savior.

Before moving ahead to discuss more fully the pneumatological and trinitarian aspects of incarnational atonement, let us turn to JBT to summarize our current course:

> God has made a Covenant *for us* in Christ (*kaine diatheke*)— nineteen hundred years before we were born. In Christ he has freely bound Himself to man, and man to Himself, in covenant love, revealing Himself as the covenant-making God ("I will be your God and you shall be my people"), and providing *for us* One in Christ, who from our side, in our name, on our behalf, as our great High Priest, has made the one true Response for us and for all men ("for us and for our children") and is our One True Offering before God.[87]

LIFTED UP INTO THE DIVINE LIFE

Asymmetrical Solidarities

> [The term Gospel] includes all the promises by which God reconciles men to Himself, and which occur throughout the Law. . . . Hence it follows that Gospel, taken in a large sense, comprehends the evidences of mercy and paternal favour which God bestowed on the patriarchs of old. In a higher sense, however, the word refers to the proclamation of the grace manifested in Christ . . . by which God fulfilled what He had promised, these promises being realised in the person of the Son. For "all the promises of God find their yea and amen in Christ" . . . because He has in His flesh completely accomplished all the parts of our salvation.—John Calvin[88]

The Torrances have been heavily influenced by John Calvin and have made major contributions in the field of Calvin studies, for example, JBT's work cited above: "The Vicarious Humanity and Priesthood of

87. JBT, "Covenant or Contract," 55.

88. Calvin, *Institutes* 2.9.2, OS 3:399–400, cited by JBT, "Vicarious Humanity and Priesthood," 79–80.

Christ in the Theology of John Calvin." For JBT, as we have seen, it is important to understand with Calvin that "all God's purposes for mankind have been brought to fulfilment in the vicarious humanity of Christ," and that "we have been renewed in the image of God in Him." Just as critical, he cautions, is remembering "the distinction between *what we are in Christ* and *what we are in ourselves.*" For instance, Calvin states, "although in ourselves polluted, we are priests in him." Regardless of the truth of our solidarity with Christ, to deny who we are in ourselves would be to fall prey to an overrealized eschatology.[89]

We are then all in solidarity with Christ, but still plagued by our solidarity with Adam. We are all children of the light and children of the darkness, holy and blameless in Christ, evil in ourselves. Yet, as Paul takes pains to demonstrate in Romans chapter 5, the solidarities we share with Christ and with Adam are asymmetrical. Speaking from the sound perspective of a realized eschatology, we can be assured that the old person died with Christ on the cross and that we rose renewed in him, and even now we are seated with him in the heavenly realms. Who we *really* are, by virtue of creation and redemption, is beloved children of the Father. And it is by the Holy Spirit that we can live in that reality even now on earth. To use dialectical language, in this "already but not yet" existence we can, by the Spirit, increasingly become who we already are in Christ (cf. Rom 8:29; 2 Cor 3:18).

TFT once described his identity this way: "The Tom Torrance you see is full of corruption, but the real Tom Torrance is hid with Christ in God and will be revealed only when Christ comes again. He took my corrupt humanity in his Incarnation, sanctified, cleansed and redeemed it, giving it new birth, in his death and resurrection."[90] Because of the ontological union established by Christ with us, any name could validly be plugged into TFT's testimony—it is true for us all. Yet the reason TFT or any person can follow Christ in this life is because, by the Spirit, he or she *knows* it to be true. That person is a believer.

As JBT never tires of saying, it is the Holy Spirit who "lifts us up" with thankful, joyful hearts to share in Christ's sonship and the trinitarian communion. "Without Pentecost," notes JBT, "and without the sealing of the Holy Spirit in faith, we cannot regard ourselves as members

---

89. JBT, "Vicarious Humanity and Priesthood," 80.

90. TFT, *Mediation of Christ*, 86.

of Christ's Body and partakers of His blessings."[91] With Calvin we must insist that "all parts of our salvation are complete in Christ," but also in quoting Calvin we can say that "until our minds are intent on the Spirit, Christ is in a manner unemployed, because we view him coldly without us, and so at a distance from us." This is in no way to dismiss the incarnational union established in Christ, says JBT, only to assert rather that "the ontological relation that we already have with Christ in virtue of His High Priesthood (expounded in Book 2) must have its counterpart in the pneumatological relation (expounded in Book 3), described in the New Testament as the sealing of the Holy Spirit."[92]

One of JBT's favorite themes in this connection is the "three moments" of salvation:

> Three answers can be given to the question of when I became a Christian. Firstly, I have been a child of God from all eternity in the heart of the Father. Secondly, I became a child of God when Christ the Son lived, died and rose again for me long ago. Thirdly, I became a child of God when the Holy Spirit—the Spirit of adoption—sealed in my faith and experience what had been planned from all eternity in the heart of the Father and what was completed once and for all in Jesus Christ. There are three moments but only one act of salvation, just as we believe there are three persons in the Trinity, but only one God. We may never divorce any one from the other two. . . . Of these three moments, the second is the decisive one in the gospel of grace.[93]

In conjunction with Calvin's commentary above, JBT helps us to see the critical role of the Spirit in bringing us to faith and in sealing our hope in Christ. As we attempt to grasp what it means to preach and believe the gospel, a distinction between the ontological and the pneumatological aspects of our salvation can be helpful. Certainly this is especially the case during the early stages of our quest, when the fear is that an ontological explanation "by itself would lead to universalism, and obscure the New Testament teaching about faith and decision."[94]

At the same time, attempting to dissect the act of salvation into three moments could have its own fearful consequences. We must take JBT's counsel fully seriously when he adamantly insists that "we may

---

91. JBT, "Priesthood of Jesus," 172.

92. Ibid.

93. JBT, *Worship, Community*, 65.

94. JBT, "Priesthood of Jesus," 172.

never divorce any one [of the moments] from the other two." We must differentiate the Holy Spirit from the Father and the Son, but we must not leave the Holy Spirit out of the *homoousion*! Notes TFT: "Just as we must think of the incarnation of the Son and his atoning work as the Mediator between God and man as taking place within the life of God, so we must surely think of the vicarious operation of the Spirit in indivisible conjunction with the vicarious activity of Christ as falling within the life of God."[95] The birth, life, death, resurrection, and ascension of Christ was fully trinitarian in nature, and the resulting "outpouring of the Holy Spirit upon us belongs to the fulfilment of God's reconciling of the world to himself."[96]

When the Spirit came, notes TFT,

> he came as the Spirit who in Jesus has penetrated into a new intimacy with our human nature. . . . And therefore he came not as isolated and naked Spirit, but as Spirit charged with all the experience of Jesus as he shared to the full our mortal nature and weakness, and endured its temptation and grief and suffering and death, and with the experience of Jesus as he struggled and prayed, and worshipped and obeyed, and poured out his life in compassion for mankind. It is still in the Name of Jesus Christ that the Holy Spirit comes to us, and in no other name.[97]

We must remember that the Spirit of Jesus did not come to continue "a work begun by Christ and now left off by him, as if we now passed from the economy of the Son into the economy of the Spirit."[98]

It is also significant to recognize that, *consistent with the rest of the vicarious humanity of Christ*, when the Torrances speak of the Spirit being mediated by Christ at Pentecost (Acts 2:33), they speak of this in a realized, universal sense rather than in a futuristic, localized sense. "Pentecost and Calvary belong inseparably and integrally together," and have the same cosmic range.[99] TFT elaborates:

> The Holy Spirit is now freely given to us in all the fulness of his life-giving and sanctifying presence. . . . While this is true in a distinctive and intimate way only of those who believe in

95. TFT, *Mediation of Christ*, 118.
96. TFT, "Atonement," 243.
97. TFT, *Theology in Reconstruction*, 246–47.
98. Ibid., 253.
99. TFT, *Mediation of Christ*, 110.

the Lord Jesus Christ as their Saviour, it has a wider application. Just as all men, whether they know it or not, are ontologically dependent upon the humanity of Jesus Christ, so they are also ontologically dependent in a new and profounder way upon the immanent presence of the Holy Spirit who, on the ground of the atoning and reconciling work of Christ, has been poured out "upon all flesh."[100]

Our mouths hang open as we consider the awesome theological and evangelical implications for a doctrine of the Spirit that corresponds to the vicarious humanity of Jesus Christ: "It is in the *Incarnation* and the *Atonement* that we learn the secret of Pentecost," states TFT; in Christ "the closed circle of the inner life of God was made to overlap with human life, and human nature was taken up to share in the eternal communion of the Father and the Son and the Holy Spirit. . . . The inner life of the Holy Trinity which is private to God alone is extended to include human nature in and through Jesus."[101]

Because the incarnation takes place within the life of God, we are placed within the life of God by the Spirit! Our ascension in the vicarious humanity of Christ is especially in view here:

> The ascension means the exaltation of man into the life of God and on to the throne of God. . . . There we reach the goal of the incarnation. . . . We are with Jesus beside God, for we are gathered up in him and included in his own self-presentation to the Father. *This is the ultimate end of creation and redemption revealed in the Covenant of Grace and fulfilled in Jesus Christ.* . . . We ourselves are given a down-payment of that, as it were, in the gift of the Spirit bestowed on us by the ascended man from the throne of God, so that through the Spirit we may already have communion in the consummated reality which will be fully actualized in us in the resurrection and redemption of the body.[102]

---

100. TFT, "Goodness and Dignity," 321.

101. TFT, *Theology in Reconstruction*, 241. Emphasis mine.

102. TFT, *Space, Time and Resurrection*, 135–36. Continues TFT: "A warning should be given at this point on the danger of *vertigo* that quickly overwhelms some people when they think of themselves as being exalted in Christ to partake of the divine nature. One finds a form of this vertigo also in some mystics and pantheists who tend to identify their own ultimate being with the divine Being. This would be the exact antithesis of what the Christian Gospel teaches, for the exaltation of man into sharing the divine life and love, affirms the reality of his humble creaturely being, by making him live out of the transcendence of God in and through Jesus alone."

Theosis Revisited

If our incarnational union with Christ has been disregarded by most in today's church, how much more so this idea that in Christ by the Spirit we have been gathered into the life of God. Yet that is exactly where the doctrine of the *homoousion* leads us. TFT points out that "the Greek Fathers were deeply influenced by the teaching of Jesus that the Scriptures 'called gods (*theoi*) those to whom the Word of God (*Logos//Theou*) came.'"[103] Hence the concept of *theosis* expressed by Athanasius: "He was made man that we might be made divine."[104] Athanasius had in mind here the glorious reality that in Christ we are made partakers of the divine nature (2 Pet 1:4), "the fact that in Jesus Christ the Son of God has become man and thus brought us into kinship with himself."[105]

TFT knows that a return to this patristic emphasis on *theosis* can have tremendously positive repercussions in the area of evangelism. Quoting him at length as he passionately makes his case:

At this point let me plead for a reconsideration by the Reformed Church of what the Greek fathers called *theosis*. This is usually unfortunately translated *deification*, but it has nothing to do with the *divinization* of man any more than the Incarnation has to do with the humanization of God. *Theosis* was the term the Fathers used to emphasize the fact that through the Spirit we have to do with God in his utter sublimity, his sheer Godness or holiness; creatures though we are, men on earth, in the Spirit we are made to participate in saving acts that are abruptly and absolutely divine, election, adoption, regeneration or sanctification, and we participate in them by grace alone. *Theosis* describes man's involvement in such a mighty act of God upon him that he is raised up to find

---

103. TFT, "Soul and Person," 112–13. Jesus' reference is to Ps 82:6.

104. Cited in TFT, *Trinitarian Faith*, 188. Cf. 189, and note how Irenaeus is not hesitant to include the Spirit in the atoning exchange: "The Lord has redeemed us through his own blood, giving his soul for our souls, and his flesh for our flesh, and has poured out the Spirit of the Father for the union and communion of God and man, imparting indeed God to men by means of the Spirit, and on the other hand attaching man to God by his own incarnation, and bestowing upon us at his coming immortality durably and truly through communion with God."

105. Ibid., 189. Paraphrasing Athanasius *Orationes contra Arianos* 1.38–39. Cf. TFT, *Theology in Reconciliation*, 231, where TFT notes that the soteriology of Athanasius was not simply *theosis*: his "conception of salvation by sanctifying exaltation and *theosis* through the Incarnation of the Word or Son of God is structured together with conceptions of atoning expiation, priestly propitiation, and substitutionary sacrifice and victory over the forces of evil, which together constitute what he means by redemption."

the true centre of his existence not in himself but in Holy God, where he lives and moves and has his being in the uncreated but creative energy of the Holy Spirit. . . .

> . . . *Theosis* is an attempt to express the staggering significance of Pentecost as the coming from on high, from outside of us and beyond us, of divine power, or rather as the coming of Almighty God, the Maker of heaven and earth, to dwell with sinful mortal man, and therefore as the emancipation of man from imprisonment in himself and the lifting of him to partake of the living presence and saving acts of God the Creator and Redeemer. Is there anything we need to regain more than this faith in the utter Godness of God the Holy Spirit?[106]

As we contemplate TFT's plea and consider the implications of *theosis* for evangelical persuasion, it might be helpful to take a step back and come at it another way. It is because of the unity of Father, Son, and Holy Spirit that we can speak of our existence being gathered into God and at the same time speak of Christ being the *center* of our existence. If our paradigm is one of Newtonian (or Arian!) space-matter dualism, roadblocks will come up regarding our being *in* Christ via incarnational union. According to this view, "If God Himself is the infinite Container of all things He can no more become incarnate than a box can become one of the several objects that it contains."[107] We are reminded of Arias's question, "How can a man praying to God himself be God?" Theologically, it is critical that we attempt to think of Jesus Christ on two planes at the same time, what TFT calls "an inter-level synthesis":

> Neither an approach to Jesus starting from his humanity, nor an approach starting from his deity, is in place: we must approach Jesus simultaneously on both levels in the space-time field in which he and we encounter each other; from the very start of our theological interpretation, therefore, we must learn to think conjunctively of him as God and man in the one indivisible fact of Jesus Christ.[108]

Because *theosis* can be an esoteric concept, it is imperative that we return over and over again to the *homoousion* of Father and Son before branching off; we have already noted the futility of attempting

106. TFT, *Theology in Reconstruction*, 243–44.

107. TFT, *Space, Time and Incarnation*, 39.

108. TFT, "Church," 766.

to "cut behind Jesus" in order to define God or to find our spirituality. Regarding Jesus Christ as the center of our existence, TFT remarks: "The Incarnation is the divine-human axis which God has thrust through the center of the creation in such a way that everything in heaven and earth, eternity and time, is made to revolve around it."[109]

As TFT insinuates here, if we are going to understand *theosis* in its applications for ministry today, we must move forward from our basis of the Father-Son *homoousion*. To properly regard Jesus Christ as the axis of the world, we must not think of the transcendent God's visit in Christ as a temporary or localized episode, like a knife plunged through the middle of an orange and pulled back out again. By endeavoring to grasp the transcendent *and* immanent truth of Jesus Christ, we are getting closer to developing a trinitarian understanding of the *homoousion*. Again we turn to TFT:

> This relation established between God and man in Jesus Christ constitutes Him as the place in all space and time where God meets with man in the actualities of his human existence, and man meets with God and knows Him in His own divine Being. That is the place where the vertical and horizontal dimensionalities intersect, the place where human being is opened out to a transcendent ground in God and where the infinite Being of God penetrates into our existence and creates room for Himself within the horizontal dimensions of finite being in space and time. It is penetration of the horizontal by the vertical that gives man his true place, for it relates his place in space and time to its ultimate ontological ground so that it is not submerged in the endless relativities of what is merely horizontal. Without this vertical relation to God man has no authentic place on the earth, no meaning and no purpose, but with this vertical relation to God his place is given meaning and purpose. For that reason it is defined and established as place on earth without being shut in on itself solely within its horizontal dimensionality. Unless the eternal breaks into the temporal and the boundless being of God breaks into the spatial existence of man and takes up dwelling within it, the vertical dimension vanishes out of man's life and becomes quite strange to him—and man loses his place under the sun.[110]

109. TFT, "Goodness and Dignity," 321.
110. TFT, *Space, Time and Incarnation*, 75–76.

Jesus Christ in the Holy Spirit established a vertical-horizontal, or a transcendent-immanent, matrix of existence for humankind. Now we are beginning to understand TFT's earlier statement that in Christ "the closed circle of the inner life of God was made to overlap with human life," and that we have been folded into the trinitarian relations. We are beginning to grasp why Paul would adopt a line from a Greek playwright in his sermon on the Areopagus: "In him we live and move and have our being" (Acts 17:28). All this is by virtue of the interconnection between incarnation and Pentecost, the critical *homoousion* between Son and Spirit. "The Word became flesh and made his dwelling among us" (John 1:14), and he still dwells among us by his Spirit; God is "over all and through all and in all" (Eph 4:6). The glorious truth of our existence is not only that the river of life runs through our world, but that we are *in* the river, whether we know it or not.

Why have we resisted reading the Scriptures this way for so long? Are we afraid of pantheism or of becoming an impersonal drop in the ocean of divine substance? Are we afraid of the scandalous idea that God dwells in and through all things by the Spirit? It could be said that it is awfully audacious to claim that the Spirit permeates even the evil villains of our world, but is that so hard to believe if we consider the oneness of Son and Spirit and the humble condescension of the Creator who took on corrupt flesh, touched leprous "sinners," was spat upon by his creatures, and at Calvary plumbed the most insidious depths of humanity's alienation from God?

Maybe it is time we stepped out of the snare of Newtonian dualism and moved past a container view of the Holy Spirit. For so long we in the evangelical community have talked in terms of the Spirit being *in* or *out* based on *our* decision to ask Christ "in," as if once he is "in," our behavior will be decreasingly evil. Common sense should make it clear that this container view does not hold water, for as believers we have to consider from a theological perspective the evil behavior of our warm-hearted, godly preacher who ran off with another's spouse, not to mention our own evildoings. We cannot ignore our solidarity with Adam and the claim sin has, however unfounded, on our lives. It is time to return theologically to the *homoousion* of Father, Son, and Holy Spirit and to consider the overriding significance of our solidarity with the Second Adam, who has staked a higher claim than the first—Jesus Christ, who has bought us and brothered us.

From the perspective of the Christian faith we are all created to be spiritual beings. I mean this not in a Platonic sense, for we believe not in the immortality of the soul but in the resurrection of the body. Our "spirit" is who we are as whole persons, and it is dependent upon the Spirit of God. It is our whole being that has been wholly gathered up and converted into the wholeness of God our Savior. Often oblivious to this fact, yet recognizing the transcendent existence of someone or something "out there," humans have been prone to wander away from our center and to attempt spiritual development independent of the Spirit of Christ, the one in whom all things hold together. Comments TFT:

> The human "spirit" is essentially a dynamic correlate of the divine "Spirit." . . . The "spirit" of man, therefore, is not something he possesses in himself as an ingredient or potency in his make-up, or as a "spark of the divine," but the ontological qualification of his soul, and indeed of his whole creaturely being, brought about and maintained by the Holy Spirit, in virtue of which he lives and moves and has his being in God, as man made in his image and likeness.[111]

Having emphasized the concept of *theosis* so strongly, I must at the same time hasten to reject any equation of this "ontological qualification" of humanity with universalism. Here we will return briefly to John Calvin, with whom we began this section. Calvin certainly had no problem with the immanence of the Spirit in and through all of the created order, including even "the impious, who are utterly estranged from God." However, Calvin held that God moves in believers in a special way.[112] For this reason, he readily endorsed the patristic notion of *theosis*. For Calvin, notes Carl Moser, "Christ unites believers to God because in his person God and humanity are already united."[113] Just as we must

---

111. TFT, "Soul and Person," 110.

112. Calvin, *Institutes* 2.11.16.

113. Moser, "Greatest Possible Blessing," 46. How Christ can be really and actually united to all persons via the incarnation and yet how some people seemingly never come to faith is a mystery Calvin may have tried too hard to solve. On Calvin's endorsement of *theosis*, Moser comments: "It must be remembered that deification is a part of the catholic tradition that Calvin and the other Reformers inherited, affirmed and defended. . . . More often than not deification in Calvin is presupposed as background rather than explicitly in the foreground" (55–56), and "though not as bold as the Church fathers sometimes are, Calvin's understanding of deification is simply the patristic notion of *theosis*" (56).

interpret all of Christ's human acts out of his being as God, we must also recognize that all of our acts toward God must be from within the being of God, from within our ontological union with God. For, whether we know it or not, unless we are first ontologically united to Jesus Christ by the Spirit, we cannot come to faith—we have no ground from which to believe. When the eyes of our hearts are opened and we come to faith, we no longer regard Christ as "coldly without us." Instead, "the Spirit himself testifies with our spirit that we are God's children" (Rom 8:16). This will be the topic of the next section.

For the sake of healthy proclamation of the gospel I am convinced that TFT is right in urging the evangelical community to reconsider the concept of *theosis* as a bolder, uncaged theology of the Spirit, one that complements the ontological union accomplished for all humankind in the birth, life, death, resurrection, and ascension of Jesus Christ. We must continue to insist that *theosis* does not have anything to do with pantheism, spiritualism, universalism, or with literal deification or divinization, a dissolving of humanity into God. It is simply a robust theology of the Holy Trinity as revealed uniquely in Immanuel, the Son of Man who received the Spirit from the Father for our sakes and subsequently poured that very Spirit out on all flesh (Acts 2:17). As we turn to address more specifically the implications of ontological, trinitarian theology for personal response to the gospel, we can confidently conclude this discussion with TFT:

> Through the historical and crucified Jesus we really meet with the risen and ascended Lord, we really meet with God in his transcendent glory and majesty, and we really are gathered into the communion of the Son with the Father and of the Father with the Son, and really are taken up through the Spirit to share in the divine life and love that have overflowed to us in Jesus Christ.
>
> . . . Through the Spirit Christ is nearer to us than we are to ourselves, and we who live and dwell on earth are yet made to sit with Christ "in heavenly places," partaking of the divine nature in him.[114]

---

114. TFT, *Space, Time and Resurrection*, 134–35.

RESPONDING TO THE GOSPEL

The Christ of Our Experience

So what can we say concerning the place of faith and belief in the gospel—have these been undermined by an ontological emphasis? At the end of the last section we considered the dangers of separating act from being, and the futility of trying to respond to God from outside the incarnational union he has established with us. As humbling as it may be to us Western rugged individualists, God has determined that we cannot make a proper response to God on our own. The Word became flesh and made his dwelling among us so that he might respond *to* God as a human being on our behalf. If we step out of what we have called the double movement of grace, the God-humanward and the human-Godward activity of Jesus Christ, it can only be like striving against the wind. Yet to respond to God within the vicarious humanity of Christ is to have the wind at our backs. Certainly this is what Paul means in Ephesians when he says, "For it is by grace you have been saved, through faith—and this is not from yourselves, it is the gift of God—not by works, so that no one can boast" (2:8, 9). Paul is saying that even our personal faith occurs within the double movement of grace. Let us continue to probe the nuances of this grace-faith relation.

JBT has noted that "the prime purpose of the incarnation, in the love of God, is to lift us up into a life of communion, of participation in the very triune life of God."[115] We have traveled this course in the last section, but the key word here is *participation*. Participation is a word used relentlessly by the Torrances, because they are convinced that everything human beings do toward God begins with God and ends with God. Because of the vicarious humanity of Christ, the fact that Christ has stood in for us, on our behalf and in our place, means that all of our responses to God are secondary; the primary response has been and continues to be given by our brother Jesus in his ascended humanity. "*Participation* is thus an important word," says JBT; "it holds together what WE do, and that in which we are given to participate."[116]

Before looking at the transformational impact of the participation concept for preaching and responding to the gospel, let us spotlight the weaknesses of what the Torrances call the "existential" model. The prob-

---

115. JBT, *Worship, Community*, 21.
116. JBT, "Vicarious Humanity and Priesthood," 145.

lem with this model, comments JBT, is that "although it stresses the God-manward movement in Christ, *the man-Godward movement is still ours!* It emphasises *our* faith, *our* decision, *our* response in an event theology which short-circuits the vicarious humanity of Christ and belittles union with him."[117] In this approach, the deity of Christ is presented strongly, but the humanity of Christ is usually presented largely as a means to an end—a way to get Jesus to the cross so the world can be saved by the extravagant, gracious *act* of God. The existential model "makes religious experience, the experience of redemption, its dogmatic starting point and central concern, and interprets the Work of Christ in terms of human need and experience, and then seeks to interpret Christ's person in terms of his Work, Christology in terms of soteriology."[118]

This existential, or "experience," model is the most pervasive in the church today, notes JBT. Many people have made decisions for Christ in this paradigm, but that does not mean that it is the most theologically sound. JBT illustrates with this story:

> A few years ago when I was lecturing in California, a student said to me: "What is wrong with that model? That is me! I was converted two years ago and gave my life to Christ." I replied that, as I saw it, there was nothing wrong in it as a description of genuine evangelical experience. From New Testament times onwards, whenever the cross of Christ has been faithfully preached by Paul, John Stott or Billy Graham, people have come to faith and conversion. But do not build your theology on it![119]

What, then, are the problems with the existential model? "Stressing the work of Christ at the expense of his person can reduce the gospel to 'events' with no ontology (separate act and being) and make our religious experience of grace central," remarks JBT. "It is a failure," he continues, "not to recognize that salvation is not simply through the work of Christ (*per Christum*), but primarily given to us in his person (*in Christo*). We draw near to God our Father in and through Christ, in the communion of the Spirit."[120] In conclusion, "more important than our experience of Christ is the Christ of our experience."[121]

---

117. Ibid., 133.
118. Ibid., 134.
119. JBT, *Worship, Community*, 22.
120. Ibid., 16.
121. Ibid., 23.

TFT adds his own sharp critique of the existential decisionist approach, which he believes compromises the vicarious humanity of Christ.

> The failure to take the *homoousion* seriously has tended to throw up the notion of *event-grace*, in which the centre of gravity is translated to man's own decisions and acts, so that Pelagian notions of co-operation and co-redemption are still rife within Protestantism. This involves a failure to distinguish the objective reality of grace from the individual believer's subjective states. . . .[122]

The anthropocentric view TFT portrays engenders a synergism that is actually a kind of relativism to be avoided at all costs. That is, what Christ has done is not truly real for us until we decide that it is. The cross is reduced to an anemic *offer* of reconciliation to us in hopes that we will embrace it. In this view Christ did not accomplish salvation as our high priest who poured out his blood of the new covenant; he only procured a possibility that awaits our validation. Fully played out this means that "in the last resort our salvation depends upon our own personal or existential decision. That is the exact antithesis of the Reformed doctrine of election, which rests salvation upon the prior and objective decision of God in Christ."[123]

"Through his incarnational and atoning union with us our faith is implicated in his faith."[124] This statement by TFT transitions us into a discussion of the alternative to the existential model—what the Torrances call the "incarnational trinitarian" model. By critiquing the experiential model we have already begun sketching out the picture of the other, but it may be helpful to delineate what the Torrances mean by "objective" and "subjective" in this context. By objective they mean what has happened in Christ, which *includes* the subjective human response of Jesus Christ on our behalf. Objective, then, is the God-humanward and human-Godward movement "in a package." Subjective could mean the subjective response of Jesus as a man in his vicarious humanity (the primary human-Godward movement), or it may mean *our* subjective response in a *participatory* way.[125] To help us to differentiate between

122. TFT, *Theology in Reconstruction*, 190.

123. Ibid., 162.

124. TFT, *Mediation of Christ*, 84.

125. Cf. *Theology in Reconstruction*, 160, where TFT describes the objective-subjective aspects of justification: "Justification has been fulfilled subjectively as well as

Jesus' Response, which is always primary, and our response, which is always secondary, the Torrances will often use the same word with upper- and lowercase letters, as I have done here.

To begin with, it must be noted that most people who have come to faith, responding as best they knew how to a gospel preached by godly preachers, had no earthly idea about the double movement of grace or the vicarious humanity of Christ. Nonetheless, it is my belief with the Torrances that all believers have come to faith, whether they realize it or not, from within that movement, from within the incarnational union that we have been discussing. I believe that a more thorough theological understanding of the truth of the gospel can only help bolster the faith of believers and embolden gospel proclaimers.

As I have mentioned, outside of humans' solidarity with Christ, they have no ground for proper response to God or for a restoration of filial relations with God. Human beings, asserts TFT, "have become so inextricably curved in upon themselves in the roots of their being, that no matter how much they exercise their free-will, they are quite unable to escape from their self-will."[126] Again, operating on the basis of a radical dualism between God and the world, this outlook, which is about "God and me" and thus without any ontological footing, only "throws the religious subject back upon his own *sacro egoismo*."

> This is a condition from which he is unable to extricate himself, since it is precisely from himself that he requires to be delivered. It is only Jesus Christ who can do that, for He is the one point in our human and historical existence where we may be lifted up out of ourselves and escape the self-incarcerating processes of human subjectivism.[127]

Incarnational trinitarian faith calls for a "critical reorientation of faith" as it is normally understood, "a repentant self-denial of its own subjectivity."[128] Only then can faith have its "full place," asserts TFT:

> It is not enough to say that the primary emphasis is upon the initiatives and the work of God, and that the subsidiary emphasis is upon the response of faith. Even if my salvation depends on God for ninety-nine percent of its efficacy and only one percent on

objectively in Jesus Christ, but that objective and subjective justification is objective to us."

126. TFT, "Goodness and Dignity," 312.

127. TFT, *God and Rationality*, 55.

128. TFT, "Place of Christology," 20.

me, my salvation is nevertheless as uncertain as my own frailty and weakness. The strength of the chain is to be measured by its weakest link.[129]

Humans are not made to take the responsibility of initiating or sustaining their own faith. TFT bemoans the fact that "in too much preaching of Christ the ultimate responsibility is taken off the shoulders of the Lamb of God and put on the shoulders of the poor sinner, and he knows well in his heart he cannot cope with it."[130] Throwing the hearer "back on himself" (one of the Torrances' favorite expressions) ignores the fact that the only acceptable response has already been provided on our behalf! Notes JBT: "Whatever else our faith is, it is a response to a Response already made for us and continually being made for us in Christ, the pioneer of our faith."[131] TFT elaborates on this idea of Jesus being "at once God's Word to man, and at the same time the Man of faith":[132]

> That is what the Word of God proclaims to us in the Gospel, and therefore it summons us to respond by faith only as it holds out to us free participation in the faithful response of Christ already made on our behalf. Hence our response of faith is made within the ring of faithfulness which Christ has already thrown around us, when in faith we rely not on our own believing but wholly on His vicarious response of faithfulness toward God. In this way Christ's faithfulness undergirds our feeble and faltering faith and enfolds it in His own; but since His faithfulness enshrines within itself the faithfulness of God and the faithfulness of the Man Jesus, we are unable to disentangle our acts of faith in Christ from their implication in the eternal faithfulness of God.[133]

It might be said that TFT was a forerunner of those who have currently adopted the subjective-genitive stance in the hot debate over the meaning of "the faith of Jesus Christ" in the Pauline corpus. TFT is of the view, substantiated by the more recent work of Richard Hays, Douglas Campbell, and others, that Galatians 2:20 should be translated: "I am crucified with Christ: nevertheless I live, yet not I but Christ lives in me; and the life which I live in the flesh I live by faith, the *faithfulness* of the

---

129. TFT, *Conflict and Agreement*, 2:129–30.

130. TFT, *Preaching Christ Today*, 35.

131. JBT, *Worship, Community*, 18.

132. JBT, "Priesthood of Jesus," 165.

133. TFT, *God and Rationality*, 154.

Son of God who loved me and gave himself for me."[134] These words, TFT reflects, "give succinct expression to the evangelical truth we have been trying to clarify. . . . *I yet not I but Christ.* This applies even to faith." He continues:

> I am convinced that the peculiar expression which St Paul uses to express the faith-relationship with Christ should be translated as I have rendered it, but even if it is translated as "by faith in the Son of God," the self-correction made by St Paul applies, "not I but Christ." That is the message of the vicarious humanity of Jesus Christ on which the Gospel tells me I may rely: that Jesus Christ in me believes in my place and at the same time takes up my poor faltering and stumbling faith into his . . . , embracing, upholding and undergirding it through his invariant faithfulness. That is the kind of faith that will not fail.[135]

TFT is quick to point out that to acknowledge Christ's response on our behalf, as comprehensive as it is, "is not in any way to denigrate the human act of faith on our part, for it is only in and through the vicarious faith of Christ that we can properly believe."[136] We must then think of Jesus Christ as "the great Believer—vicariously believing in our place and in our name."[137] As such, he is "the embodiment of our salvation . . . , the anchor of our hope."[138]

"Christ is your life." That is what Paul told the Colossians (3:3-4), but it is a truism not easily received. Our sinful tendency is to react, "No, I've got my own life." We go to great lengths to protect our prized individual agency; with zero-sum logic, we are fearful of our lives being diminished. Instead, by participating in the life of our Creator-Redeemer, we are enlarged into the purposes of our created and colorful particularity. Our Savior reminded us that to lose one's life is to find it; it is when we give up our individual agency, and the right to have the last word, that we find our most personal and free response to God. We find it in the Person who has already found us. This is the comfort of the gospel.

---

134. TFT, *Mediation of Christ*, 98. Concerning TFT as a forerunner, see his subjective-genitive stance in "One Aspect." Cf. Hays, "PISTIS and Pauline Christology"; Campbell, *Rhetoric of Righteousness*.

135. TFT, *Mediation of Christ*, 98.

136. TFT, *Preaching Christ Today*, 31.

137. TFT, *Theology in Reconstruction*, 157.

138. TFT, "One Aspect," 114.

In the words of Karl Barth: "*In Jesus Christ God has bound Himself to us and bound us to Himself before ever we have bound ourselves to Him.*"[139]

With their Barthian foundation and its accompanying insistence on the thoroughness of Christ's mediation for us, it is no surprise that the Torrances are troubled by the subtle Pelagianism they detect in much modern preaching—"the way people often preach the gospel and claim that people will be saved only if they believe, or on condition that they believe."[140] They are baffled by the idea of salvation through faith alone, "where 'faith alone' may mean 'mere faith' as if to be regenerated were simply resolvable into believing."[141] Replacing the primary Response of Christ with our own subjective response of faith or belief has dire consequences for our theology of the cross and in the area of assurance, which is vital for sanctification in Christ, as we shall continue to see.

Justification by Grace through Faith

"It is justification by grace that guards the gospel from corruption," asserts TFT.[142] As we attempt to unpack this statement, we must critically assess the oft-confused language of justification by grace and justification by faith. What exactly is the difference between these two concepts? First, a word about the term *justification*. In the Bible, *to justify* means *to put in the right*, or *to put in the truth*. The staggering message of the gospel concerns "the justification of the ungodly," and that is what God accomplished when he exposed humans as guilty and made us righteous in Jesus Christ. He put sinners in the right. [143] As we considered earlier regarding belief, Jesus Christ has fulfilled the God-humanward and the human-Godward sides of justification:

> In that unity of the divine and the human, justification was fulfilled in Christ from both sides, from the side of the justifying God and from the side of justified man—"He was justified in the Spirit," as St Paul put it. Justification as objective act and justifi-

---

139. Barth, *Church Dogmatics* 2/2 §39, quoted by TFT, *Conflict and Agreement*, 2:123. Italics mine.

140. TFT, *Preaching Christ Today*, 37.

141. TFT, *Theology in Reconstruction*, 180.

142. Ibid., 162.

143. Ibid., 153.

cation as subjective actualization of it in our estranged human existence have once and for all taken place—in Jesus.[144]

"Through union with him we share in his faith, in his obedience, in his trust and appropriation of the Father's blessing; we share in his justification before God."[145] The justification of Jesus Christ does not only forgive our sins, as in wiping out the debit column or balancing the books; rather than simply negating the negative, it actually generates or inspires a "positive righteousness" that involves a "perpetual living in Christ, from a centre and source beyond us. To be justified is to be lifted up above and beyond ourselves to live out of the risen and ascended Christ, and not out of ourselves."[146] Although we cannot linger over it here, the immensity of what Christ has accomplished for us in his vicarious humanity helps us to keep justification and sanctification together instead of dividing them into two separate stages of Christian experience. A thought from TFT will suffice:

> Justification by grace alone remains the sole ground of the Christian life; we never advance beyond it, as if justification were only the beginning of a life of sanctification which is what we do in response to justification. Of course we are summoned to live out day by day what we already are in Christ through his self-consecration or sanctification, but sanctification is not what we do in addition to what God has done in justification.[147]

Because God has done it all, "justification by faith" must be understood only as a corollary to "justification by grace." It is true that we often use these phrases to mean the same thing, that is, justification *not* by works. We must not, however, understand "justification by faith" to mean that we are not justified until we have faith! That would make faith itself a work, something we have to do to be right with God.

> Therefore when we are justified by faith, this does not mean that it is our faith that justifies us, far from it—it is the faith of Christ alone that justifies us, but we in faith flee from our own acts even of repentance, confession, trust and response, and take refuge in the

144. Ibid., 157.
145. Ibid., 159.
146. Ibid., 152–53.
147. Ibid., 161–62.

obedience and faithfulness of Christ—"Lord I believe, help thou mine unbelief." That is what it means to be justified by faith.[148]

How consoling and invigorating for the believer to be able to say with Paul, "The just shall live by faith"—knowing that the primary reference is to the faithfulness of God in Jesus Christ.[149] "Whenever there is talk of 'justifying faith,'" however, "then uncertainty creeps in, for all our acts . . . are unworthy before God. If it is upon our repentance and our faith that we have ultimately to rely, who can be saved, not to speak of being sure of his salvation?"[150]

When we distill "justification by faith alone" and "justification by grace alone" down to their lowest common denominator, what we get is purely this—Jesus Christ; Jesus Christ as the gospel of grace, "for grace is none other than Christ."[151] Now we see it all coming together; we see that the God-humanward/human-Godward movement of grace, this "package" we have been talking about, *is* Jesus Christ!

> What God communicates to us in his grace is none other than himself. The Gift and the Giver are one. Grace is not something that can be detached from God . . . ; nor is it something that can be proliferated in many forms; nor is it something we can have more or less of, as if grace could be construed in quantitative terms. This is the Reformation doctrine of *tota gratia*. Grace is whole and indivisible because it is identical with the personal self-giving of God to us in his Son. It is identical with Jesus Christ.[152]

With the revelation that the Gift is the Giver comes an accompanying exegetical explosion. Is not this what was on Paul's mind as he penned his letters?—at the beginning: "I give thanks to God always for you because of the grace of God which was given you in Christ Jesus" (1 Cor 1:4 RSV); at the end: "The grace of the Lord Jesus Christ be with your spirit" (Phil 4:23); and everywhere in between:

> Therefore, since we have been justified through faith, we have peace with God through our Lord Jesus Christ, through whom we have gained access by faith into this grace in which we now

148. Ibid., 159.

149. TFT, *Preaching Christ Today*, 31.

150. TFT, *Theology in Reconstruction*, 161.

151. Ibid., 265.

152. Ibid., 182–83.

> stand. . . . For if the many died by the trespass of the one man, how much more did God's grace and the gift that came by the grace of the one man, Jesus Christ, overflow to the many . . . so that, just as sin reigned in death, so also grace might reign through righteousness to bring eternal life through Jesus Christ our Lord. (Rom 5:1–2, 15, 21)[153]

TFT calls Romans 3:24 "the simplest and most profound expression of grace" given by Paul: "There is no difference, for all have sinned and fallen short of the glory of God, *and are justified freely by his grace through the redemption that came by Christ Jesus.*"[154] For Paul, grace is in and through Jesus Christ. Humanity *in Christ* means humanity involved in the double movement of grace intrinsic *to* Christ. Far from being satisfied with grace as a static ontological category, Paul constantly urges his brethren to actively participate in the dynamic flow of grace given to them: "You then, my son, be strong in the grace that is in Christ Jesus" (2 Tim 2:1).

Even if, for Paul, the inner meaning of God's relations with humanity is the covenant of grace revealed in Christ, how evident is this concept in Christ's own teachings? The rare appearance of *charis* in the Gospels themselves should not confuse us, says TFT. Jesus did not have to speak about grace, for he was the embodiment of grace! "Though it is not recorded that Christ Himself ever spoke of grace, it is quite clear, as the prologue to St. John's Gospel indicates, that Christ who was 'full of grace' was the source of the whole conception."[155]

---

153. Obviously, these are only a selective sampling.

154. TFT, *Doctrine of Grace*, 28. Writes TFT: "It would be safe to say that Paul never speaks of grace, except as grounded in the self-giving of God in the person and death of Jesus."

155. Ibid., 22. TFT continues: "In this sense, too, the teaching of Christ is full of grace, and out of that fullness has the rest of the New Testament received. It is upon the person and work of Christ, therefore, that emphasis must be laid in any account of grace in the Gospels. It matters little that the word *charis* in its significant sense is wanting, for there it is not in the abstract that we encounter grace, but in concrete manifestation: in the glad spontaneous fashion in which our Lord received sinners as in the instances of Matthew and Zacchaeus, of the sinful woman in Simon's house and the woman brought before Him to be stoned, freely loving them, and in the eager compassion in which He healed the sick and suffering, as in His constant demand for mercy and forgiveness among men because of the love of God. Quite as compelling in presenting the features of grace is His teaching on the merciful and forgiving love of God, especially in parables such as the lost coin, the lost sheep, the lost son, the labourers in the vineyard, or the good Samaritan."

If for JBT the great sin of the church is to turn God's covenant of grace into a contract, perhaps we could say that for TFT "the great mistake has been to detach the thought of grace from the person of Jesus Christ."[156] To revisit TFT's statement above regarding the Gift and the Giver, detachment happens when grace is thought of as something that can be "proliferated," or "something we can have more or less of, as if grace could be construed in quantitative terms." When severance occurs between Giver and Gift, grace takes on a "pragmatic slant," as in the case of "irresistible grace," which carries "an internal connection between 'grace' and 'cause.'"[157]

It is unfortunate that Western Christendom has in large part failed to keep Giver and Gift together, and therefore missed the intrinsic meaning of grace. When we begin to use "grace" instrumentally, we also begin to use the humanity of Christ instrumentally, as a means to an end. As goes our adherence to the vicarious humanity of Christ, so goes our conception of grace, as JBT concludes:

> So it is in the Latin West that the phrase "means of grace" occurs as though God provides the means we need to find the solution to our human problems. But this can obscure the fact that grace is God giving himself to us in love in Christ, and doing for us what we cannot do for ourselves. Grace means Jesus Christ clothed with his Gospel.[158]

PREACHING THE GOSPEL

Come, Creator Spirit

May the grace of the Lord Jesus Christ, and the love of God, and the fellowship of the Holy Spirit be with you all. (2 Cor 13:14)

Upon being introduced to what the Torrances call their "evangelical theology," many believers are filled with gratitude. They recognize that they are undeserving sinners saved by grace alone and that they are not even believers in and of themselves, but only in Christ, the one true believer. Comforted and assured of their salvation and sanctification, these believers are free to live a fruitful life of participatory discipleship. They

156. Ibid., v.

157. TFT, *Theology in Reconstruction*, 172, 173.

158. JBT, "Strengths and Weaknesses of Westminster," 52.

have been convinced that God is more committed to them than they could possibly be to God, and that the Holy Spirit, always in conjunction with the ongoing vicarious high priestly ministry of Christ, is ever conforming them to the image of the Son.

At the same time, others are threatened. They feel that their personal space is being violated! They do not like the idea that their lives have been woven into the fabric of Jesus Christ in his incarnational union and vicarious humanity. These believers think of ontological solidarity as depersonalizing. Perhaps subconsciously if not consciously they want to provide a primary response to God, and not just to be relegated to participatory status.

There is another group of believers as well. Those include men and women who are leaning in to hear more of this evangelical theology. They like what they hear because it interprets God and Scripture out of God's unique revelation in Christ and therefore does not force a schism in the character of God. Believing in Jesus' words that "without me you cannot do a thing," they have no problem with the idea of playing second fiddle in all aspects of the Christian life. They welcome the robust theology of the cross that really effects reconciliation and not just its possibility, and they recognize that total grace is a total indictment against human attempts to go it alone. Not only that, they especially feel that humans' serious struggle with "original sin" is best understood within the covenant of grace—that God in his filial purposes has fundamentally been against sin, not sinners, all along. Only the theology of the asymmetrical solidarities makes sense of the sin in unbelievers and believers alike, for it forces us to depend on the Holy Spirit to live out of our true, not corrupt, selves. But the hindrance for this group comes down to the pneumatological implication of the ontological solidarity wrought by the incarnation of Jesus.

Again, the idea of *theosis* is often dismissed as heretical because many of us, especially in the West, have been acculturated to think of the Holy Spirit in container fashion, "the interiorizing in our hearts of divine salvation."[159] Pure and simple, Western conventional wisdom asserts that what makes a person a believer is whether or not he or she possesses the Spirit. We forget that the Holy Spirit is free to go where he wants, when he wants, and how he wants; that he permeates all things.

159. TFT, *Theology in Reconstruction*, 242.

We also do not notice the theological disconnect we make between the activity of Christ and the activity of the Holy Spirit when we adopt this container view. In other words, while holding to the creation and redemption of the world by Christ, we hold the Creator and Redeemer Spirit out of the equation. As we have seen in our discussion of *theosis*, it is even possible to keep the *homoousion* intact between Father and Son and between humankind and Son, effecting the wondrous exchange via the hypostatic union, yet to exclude the Spirit's *homoousion* with the Son and in turn with all of humanity.[160]

This inconsistency must be drawn out and exposed if we are to move ahead with healthy theological persuasion. For in order to preach a gospel of total grace that does not throw people back on themselves, we must have a complementary robust theology of the Holy Spirit. The alternative, at best, is to give what Christ has accomplished for our salvation objective reality but to give the Spirit only a subjectivizing role pertinent to individual decisions and existential moments. The Holy Spirit becomes a "second-class citizen" in the Trinity, "and has very little if anything to do with the objective reality of the Being and living presence and action of God himself in the world."[161]

At worst, the alternative is to turn the dynamic concept of total grace into institutionalized grace, a static, impersonal blanket of forgiveness and charity. By not asking sinners to see themselves as personally implicated in the death and life of Christ, this kind of blanket grace opens the door to antinomianism, universalism, and the like, and smothers the motivation to preach a performative gospel. This is the "cheap grace" that, as Dietrich Bonhoeffer warned, justifies the sin and not the sinner.

Let us go back to the drawing board with the Torrances in an attempt to look through the Scriptures for a theology of the Spirit that matches the person and work of Christ and will be of practical use in gospel proclama-

160. It is important to be clear about what I do and do not mean here. We can say we are *homoousios* with the Spirit in one sense but not in another. On the one hand, keeping in mind the perfect unity of the Godhead, to be one with Christ is to be one with all the persons of the Trinity. On the other hand, with the differentiation of the Father, Son, and Holy Spirit in mind, we must not say we are *homoousios* with the Spirit, because the Spirit did not share our flesh like the Son. We can say we are one with the Spirit, then, not because we are directly *homoousios* with him, but because of his direct *homoousion* with the Son and the Son's solidarity with us—our oneness with Christ in his risen humanity. That is why we can say that in Christ the Spirit is closer to us than we are to ourselves.

161. TFT, *Theology in Reconstruction*, 270.

tion. We must recall that the purpose of the incarnation and atonement is to fold humanity into the trinitarian relations—sharing by grace in the sonship of the Son, the love of the Father, and the fellowship of the Holy Spirit. Paul's benediction cited above is essentially the description of the trinitarian environment, where each person has been placed via the incarnational union and vicarious humanity of Jesus Christ.

> Jesus Christ, true God and true Man, is thus the Mediator of the Holy Spirit. Since he is himself both the God who gives and the Man who receives in one Person he is in a position to transfer in a profound and intimate way what belongs to us in our human nature to himself and to transfer what is his to our human nature in him. That applies above all to the gift of the Holy Spirit whom he received fully and completely in his human nature for us.[162]

If Christ mediated the Holy Spirit to us, it is the Holy Spirit who now comes among us to mediate Christ to humanity. "He does not come in His own Name but in the Name of the Son."[163] It is the Holy Spirit who helps us "catch up" to the reality of what Christ has accomplished on our behalf. His work is in perfect conjunction with Christ's, for as Christ united himself to us at our very worst and effected the soteriological inversion, the Spirit within us opens us up from the inside to lead us to Christ. Concerning the unique role of the Spirit, TFT comments that "with His emancipation of ourselves from ourselves He lifts us above and beyond ourselves to find the truth of our being in God."[164]

The Spirit then draws us into alignment with the human-Godward trajectory already established by Jesus for the new humanity. There is certainly an eschatological dimension to this that is difficult to articulate. Basically, TFT is saying that each person has been put in an "already but not yet" situation regarding the reality of his or her redemption, and the Spirit is the gap-closer between these two states. The Torrances refuse to attempt to solve the mystery of why the "already" does not govern the "not yet" in a logico-causal way. Suffice it to say that closing this gap artificially would fly in the face of the biblical witness, which always preserves God's freedom and the God-given freedom of human beings.

Scripturally, freedom, truth, and the Holy Spirit go together. God allows people to resist the already-truth of their lives; that is obvious.

162. Ibid., 246.
163. TFT, *God and Rationality*, 171.
164. Ibid., 174.

But such resistance is not of itself a free act; an anti-truth move is intrinsically an anti-free move. So while the Holy Spirit will never force or manipulate a person into belief, it is only in the freedom of the Holy Spirit that one may come to belief. TFT elaborates:

> Here we are concerned with a two-fold doctrine: an ontological relation between all men and the human nature of the Son, for the incarnation of the Word by whom all things were made posits a creative relation between Jesus Christ and all human being; and a personal presence of the Holy Spirit to all men sustaining and consummating their creaturely relations with God through the Word. . . . It is through the power of the Spirit that human minds are informed with the Word and enlightened with the Truth.[165]

At this point the question for evangelism becomes, If we jettison a container view of the Holy Spirit, and every person is ontologically related to Christ and the Spirit, then what new thing happens when people come to faith? Or to put it another way, how do we define personal conversion without using container language? Consider again the quotation from TFT just above, and the phrases that describe conversion in terms of finding something that is already there, having our eyes opened to the existing reality—"informed with the Word," "enlightened with the Truth." It could be said that while we are under the sound of the gospel, God "discovers himself to us."[166]

As JBT explains it, the moment we "decide for Christ," we have, by the Spirit, "caught up" with the real moment that occurred two thousand years earlier; as we give our assent and consent to the gospel, "our amen is our response in the Spirit to His Amen for us."[167] Adds TFT: "On the ground of what he has already done for us in Christ He quickens us by His Spirit."[168] Yet regardless of whether we are aware of the participatory nature of our decision, it is a real and transforming event, what the Bible calls *metanoia*.

> The Incarnation, as culminating in the Cross and the Resurrection, is the great act of God in which he entered our perverted order of nature and wrought the basic soteriological inversion by which we are reconciled to God. But that basic soteriological inversion must be pushed through the whole region of the mind, inasmuch

165. Ibid., 172.

166. TFT, *Space, Time and Resurrection*, 177.

167. JBT, "Place of Christ in Worship," 367.

168. TFT, *Conflict and Agreement*, 2:129.

as we are alienated from God, as Calvin said, "in the whole of our mental system." Therefore, "let this mind be among you which was also in Christ Jesus. . . ." That takes place in Christian *metanoia*, when the believer, transformed by the renewing of his mind, knows that he has not chosen Christ, but that Christ has chosen him; that his knowing of God is grounded on his being known of God.[169]

"By its intrinsic nature an evangelical theology is an evangelizing theology," asserts TFT, "for it is concerned with the winning and transforming of the human mind through conformity to the mind of Christ Jesus." Far from being passive in character, then, from this perspective "through preaching of the Gospel we are called to become now in ourselves what we already are in Christ."[170] Paul told the Philippians, "Work out your salvation with fear and trembling, for it is God who works in you to will and to act according to his good purpose" (Phil 2:12–13)— that is, work out what God has worked in. It is clear that "what has been realised intensively for us *in Christ* must be worked out extensively *in us* in the world, by the Holy Spirit."[171]

From within the Torrances' evangelical theology we can preach simultaneously the most bold and most assuring gospel. We preach the gospel knowing that those who are present *belong to Christ before they believe.* Of course, that truth will not make much apparent difference if proclaimed to the hard-hearted, but once the eyes of listeners' hearts are opened and they are quickened to belief, that assuring fact will help cement their faith. "He who responds to [the resurrection message] by faith discovers that he has already been involved in the resurrection and is already included in the objective reality of Jesus Christ risen from the dead."[172]

169. TFT, *Theology in Reconstruction*, 115–16.

170. JBT, "Priesthood of Jesus," 165–66.

171. Ibid., 165. In a personal interview I asked JBT about this Philippians passage, which is not included in the page cited. He agreed that it probably refers to the vicarious humanity of Christ, in light of the "Philippian Hymn" immediately preceding it, and that our working out of our salvation is a participation in that of our brother who worked out his own salvation in fear and trembling: "During the days of Jesus' life on earth, he offered up prayers and petitions with loud cries and tears to the one who could save him from death, and he was heard because of his reverent submission. Although he was a son, he learned obedience from what he suffered" (Heb 5:7–8).

172. TFT, *Space, Time and Resurrection*, 35.

What exactly does *metanoia* look like? What is the result? Through this transformational convergence of actual (ontological) and existential, believers enjoy life in the Spirit, *koinonia*, which can be translated "fellowship," "sharing," "participation."[173] With full assurance of being anchored in Christ, they know they are folded into the fellowship of God, sharing in the triune relations: "God sent the Spirit of his Son into our hearts, the Spirit who calls out, 'Abba, Father'" (Gal 4:6). With thankful hearts, believers are eager to give credit where credit is due, participating in worship and prayer in union and communion with Christ and one another. What we are describing here is the inner essence of the church. The body of Christ is made up of those desirous to "live into" the reality of Christ. As the body, it is called to be the tangible expression of what it means to follow the Head of the human race.

Because the dynamic of *koinonia* is at bottom founded on the universal truth of Christ for all people, believers are keen to get others in on the "reality party." Naturally, a holistic style of evangelism emerges that includes an ambassadorship of peace, hope, and restorative justice and that acknowledges the reconciliation of all persons to God and to one another. And it all starts with having ears to hear! In Karl Barth's words, the believer "obtains that freedom of becoming a hearer [having inner ears for the Word of Christ], a responsible, grateful, hopeful person." When that happens, says Barth, it is "not because of an act of the human spirit, but solely because of an act of the Holy Spirit."[174]

If this radical change of mind, *metanoia*, describes our experience of conversion, then what about the event language we so often use about "asking Christ in" to our lives or hearts? It would be dangerous to go around saying that Christ or the Spirit is already in everyone's heart in that way. But it would be just as foolish to say that he wasn't there before he "came in"! Both of these false perspectives reflect the kind of possessive container language we must avoid.

> In this connection Calvin used to comment upon the teaching of
> St Paul that Christ dwells in our hearts by faith, to the effect that
> while it is through faith that Christ comes to dwell in our hearts,
> his dwelling involves a relation in being beyond faith. Through

173. JBT, *Worship, Community*, 8–9.

174. Barth, *Dogmatics in Outline*, 140; within brackets, 138. Regarding Barth, his sermons to prisoners are prime examples of how to preach in the evangelical way we are discussing; see his *Call for God* and *Deliverance to the Captives*.

faith we enter in to an ontological relation between Christ as our Redeemer and Creator, for he both redeems and recreates our being in him.[175]

We must remember that the Holy Spirit and Christ by the Holy Spirit is everywhere present, he is closer to us than we are to ourselves. Seen this way, the question becomes not, "Do you have the Holy Spirit?" but, "Does the Holy Spirit have you?"

As we proclaim the gospel in such a way that we encourage people to look away from themselves to the objective realities, we pray for the Holy Spirit to blow through with power, particularizing his objective truth to individual persons. We pray the prayer *Come, Creator Spirit*:

> Along with the birth, life, death, resurrection and ascension of Christ the pouring out of his Spirit at Pentecost belongs to the series of God's mighty acts which brought salvation to mankind and inaugurated the new age. . . . We live on this side of Pentecost and are on our way to meet the Advent Christ . . . within the new age in which the Creator Spirit is abroad among men and actively at work among them in a new and distinctive way, in addition to his original and continuing operation in the world. *Come, Creator Spirit* is a prayer of participation in this new happening, a prayer in which we allow it to overtake us; it is a prayer in which we ask that the new mode of the Spirit's entry into the lives of men at Pentecost may not be obstructed in our own experience. . . . *Come, Creator Spirit* is a prayer of commitment to what God has already done in Jesus Christ, and a prayer of participation in the divine nature.[176]

Evangelical Repentance

Finally, how do the Torrances recommend preaching in a sound evangelical, as opposed to "unevangelical," manner? Preaching Jesus Christ as the gospel of grace and the ground of faith is not easy, "for when we call upon people to repent and believe in Jesus Christ that they may be saved, we have great difficulty in doing that in such a way that we do not throw people back upon themselves in autonomous acts of personal

---

175. TFT, *Theology in Reconstruction*, 180. This profound comment summarizes beautifully what the evangelical community needs to understand. Conversion is, by the Spirit, entering into something (the ontological relation) that is already there.

176. Ibid., 240, 241–42.

repentance and decision." As we have said, God must be the initiating subject and the responding subject in salvation,[177] for the chain that binds us to God is only as strong as its weakest link. If people know they are that weak link, then the gospel is not really good news unless they also know that they and their feeble responses have been totally replaced by Christ and his faithful Response.[178] "The Gospel is to be proclaimed in such a way that full place is given to the man Jesus in his Person and Work as the Mediator between God and man, otherwise it is not being proclaimed in a way that corresponds with its actual message of unconditional grace and reconciling exchange."[179]

It is the gospel of unconditional grace—that Christ has taken our place to give us his place—that calls persons completely into question, for it puts the "ax at the root" of all self-justification and exposes the desperate plight of individualism. Ego-centric people do not like being told they have been replaced! This is in line with Jesus' message "when he proclaimed that all who wished to be his disciples must renounce themselves, or give up all right to themselves, take up the cross and follow him, and when he laid it down as a basic principle that those who want to save their lives will lose them."[180]

It is critical that when we call people to repentance we do so in the proper way. We must avoid a message that proclaims, "Repent, and if you repent you will be forgiven!" notes JBT, "as though God our Father has to be conditioned into being gracious! It makes the imperatives of obedience prior to the indicatives of grace, and regards God's love and forgiveness and acceptance as conditional on what we do—upon our meritorious acts of repentance." Following Calvin, JBT warns us against putting repentance ahead of forgiveness; he calls this "unevangelical repentance." "Evangelical repentance, on the other hand, takes the form: 'Christ has borne your sins on the cross, therefore repent! Receive his forgiveness in repentance!' That is, repentance is our response to grace, not a condition of grace."[181] It is not difficult to see the consistency

---

177. Ibid., 253. "Through the coming of the Spirit God brings his self-revelation to its fulfilment, for the Spirit is the creative Subject of God's revelation to us and the creative Subject in our reception and understanding of that revelation."

178. TFT, *Mediation of Christ*, 93.

179. Ibid., 92.

180. Ibid.

181. JBT, *Worship, Community*, 44. A good example of this approach is in Acts

between the idea of evangelical repentance and the unconditional covenant of grace established by God from the beginning. In a memorable illustration JBT discusses evangelical repentance:

> If two people have the misfortune to quarrel, and one comes to the other and says, in all sincerity: "I forgive you!" it is clearly not only a word of love and reconciliation, but also a word (perhaps a withering word) of condemnation—for in pronouncing his forgiveness, he is clearly implying that the other party is the guilty party! . . . Sensing the element of judgment, of condemnation in the word, [the other] might well reject the forgiveness, because he refuses to submit to the verdict of guilty implied in it. He would be impenitent. There would be no change of heart. But, suppose on subsequent reflection he comes back to his friend and says: "You were quite right! I was in the wrong!" Implicit in his acceptance of love and forgiveness he would be submitting to the verdict of guilty. There would be a real change of mind, an act of penitence on his part (*metanoia*), conversion, reconciliation.[182]

Is not this reflective of what we see in Scripture when Paul, after spending eleven chapters in Romans outlining the good news of Jesus Christ as the gospel of grace, pleads with his hearers to accept God's forgiveness in repentance?[183] "With eyes wide open to the mercies of God, I beg you, my brothers, as an act of intelligent worship, to give Him your bodies as a living sacrifice, consecrated to Him and acceptable by Him" (Rom 12:1 JBP). And likewise Paul preaches the reconciling exchange and evangelical repentance to the Corinthians:

> God was reconciling the world to himself in Christ, not counting men's sins against them. And he has committed to us the message of reconciliation. We are therefore Christ's ambassadors, as though God were making his appeal through us. We implore you on Christ's behalf: Be reconciled to God. God made him who had no sin to be sin for us, so that in him we might become the righteousness of God. (2 Cor 5:19–21)

---

chapter 2, where Peter tells the gospel story of the man Jesus of Nazareth, crucified and now raised to the right hand of the Father, where he has poured out the Holy Spirit on all people. Luke narrates that when the people heard this, "they were cut to the heart and said, '. . . What shall we do?'" Peter tells them to repent and be baptized for the forgiveness of their sins. He is not saying that if they repent and are baptized they will be forgiven. He is telling them to repent and walk in the truth of their forgiveness—to submit to the verdict of guilty implied in the cross, where they at once have been loved, condemned, and forgiven in Christ.

182. Ibid., 45.

183. JBT, "Place of Christ in Worship," 349.

From the passages cited above, it is plain that proper theological persuasion involves begging, appealing, imploring people to receive God's forgiveness in repentance. And we as Christ's ambassadors can know that we preach, yet not we but Christ who lives in us, "as though God were making his appeal through us."

Old proclamation habits die hard. Yet surely the time and energy taken by gospel preachers for rigorous reorientation toward "evangelical" witness would be worth the effort. Whether or not we paste the following schematic example to the inside front cover of our sermon preparation notebooks, the scriptural truths TFT has included in it must be continually reinforced if we are to be faithful ambassadors for Christ now and in subsequent generations.

> We preach and teach the gospel evangelically, then, in such a way as this: God loves you so utterly and completely that he has given himself for you in Jesus Christ his beloved Son, and has thereby pledged his very Being as God for your salvation. In Jesus Christ God has actualised his unconditional love for you in your human nature in such a once for all way, that he cannot go back upon it without undoing the Incarnation and the Cross and thereby denying himself. Jesus Christ died for you precisely because you are sinful and utterly unworthy of him, and has thereby already made you his own before and apart from your ever believing in him. He has bound you to himself by his love in a way that he will never let you go, for even if you refuse him and damn yourself in hell his love will never cease. Therefore, repent and believe in Jesus Christ as your Lord and Saviour. From beginning to end what Jesus Christ has done for you he has done not only as God but as man. He has acted in your place in the whole range of your human life and activity, including your personal decisions, and your responses to God's love, and even your acts of faith. He has believed for you, fulfilled your human response to God, even made your personal decision for you, so that he acknowledges you before God as one who has already responded to God in him, who has already believed in God through him, and whose personal decision is already implicated in Christ's self-offering to the Father, in all of which he has been fully and completely accepted by the Father, so that in Jesus Christ you are already accepted by him. Therefore, renounce yourself, take up your cross and follow Jesus as your Lord and Saviour.[184]

---

184. TFT, *Mediation of Christ*, 94.

CONCLUSION: KEEPING GRACE AND TRUTH TOGETHER

*All over the world this gospel is bearing fruit and growing, just as
it has been doing among you since the day you heard it and understood God's grace in all its truth.* (Col 1:6)

We have come to the end of our journey. In a sense, while building a foundation for theological persuasion, we have never left the question with
which we began, Who is Jesus Christ? We have looked at the intrinsic
significance of Jesus Christ, what he has accomplished in his person, and
how by the Spirit we may participate in that reality by responding to and
preaching Jesus Christ as the gospel of grace and the ground of faith.

What will gospel proclamation look like as we move further into
the twenty-first century? It is my conviction that the onto-relational
evangelical theology espoused by Tom and James Torrance is going to
be instrumental in presenting "Jesus Christ and him crucified" to what
has been termed post-Christian or postmodern culture. When it comes
to getting a full picture of who Jesus Christ is and what he has accomplished in his person, "the loss of ontology has been quite fatal"[185] for the
church. The "modern mind," comments TFT, "lacks ontological depth.
Somehow the top of our existence seems to be severed from its roots in
a deeper level of reality, so that it lacks a consistent substructure to hold
it together."[186]

To use the above phrase as an example, "Jesus Christ" (being) has
been separated from "him crucified" (act). Then, as we have seen, in
Newtonian dualistic fashion incarnation is severed from atonement,
revelation from reconciliation, Christology from soteriology, Giver from
Gift, Creator from Redeemer—and the repercussions for proclamation
are devastating. Thankfully, it appears that ontology might be making
a comeback, although the logico-causalities are always up for a fight in
their efforts to demystify the gospel. Perhaps we will finally jettison spa-
tial container views in favor of a multilevel synthesis way of thinking,
gaining a greater appreciation for act by putting it back within being,
the work of Christ back within his person, the believing of humans back
within their belonging to God.

I have argued that it was right for the Greek fathers to eye the ontological emphasis in Holy Scripture, a perspective that was obscured in

185. TFT, "Church," 768.
186. Ibid., 763.

the Middle Ages and only partly retrieved in the Reformation. In order to go forward theologically we will need to move backward to classical patristic theology, "the theology most relevant to the post-Einsteinian world, although it needs to be recast in the idiom and style of our own era."[187] Here we will re-appreciate the *homoousion* that establishes the trinitarian union, the hypostatic union, and the incarnational or reconciling union, all of which together ground the incarnation of Jesus Christ in the being of God and us as well via our solidarity with him and his vicarious humanity. It is from within his love that we can respond to his love. It was Pascal who profoundly imagined these words of God: "You would not seek me if you had not found me."

In regard specifically to proclamation, I would contend that the word *truth* is uniquely suited to an articulation of the gospel in this day and age. While the postmodern generation is prone to reject all dogmatic truth claims, we find in Jesus Christ that truth has dynamic and intrinsic significance. Because Jesus Christ is God being true to himself, there is a coinherence of act and being. While this is seen in the Pauline conception of grace (the double movement of grace), it is even more easily seen in *truth* when we think of truth not as some "abstract or metaphysical truth" but as "the reality of God in covenant relationship"[188]—"I will keep truth with you; therefore you keep truth with me."

I have made the contention that Jesus Christ is grace in his person for the reasons just mentioned, but in Jesus' own words we have recorded "I am truth." Jesus Christ is "uncreated Truth and created truth in one . . . , Truth of God and the answering truth of man. . . . Jesus Christ is the actualization of the Truth of God among us in such a way that it creates its own counterpart in us to itself." It is the resurrection that functions as the validation of this actualization. "If the resurrection did not take place, then not only is there a final disjunction between God's Word and God's Act, e.g. in the forgiveness of our sins, but inevitably a final disjunction between our acts of knowing and the reality of God himself."[189]

---

187. Ibid., 755.

188. TFT, "One Aspect," 112. The LXX word for *truth* is *aletheia*, which gives the latter (dynamic) connotation. This interpretation also complements the Hebrew word *'emeth*, which "is applied above all to God's Word, for when His deed corresponds to His Word, that is Truth. Truth is the faithfulness between God's actions and His Word" (112).

189. TFT, *Space, Time and Resurrection*, 71.

By virtue of the incarnation and atonement, "Truth is done into our flesh and blood." Yes, the Christian "has a relation to the Truth which Paul calls 'communion' and which John calls 'abiding.'"[190] But with this we must always remember that while believers are participating in the truth, they are not making the truth more true by their participation! In other words, they are not completing the truth or adding to the truth. No, reminds TFT, "It is in Jesus Christ, therefore, and in him alone, that the real truth of human nature is to be found, for in him God has made good his original claim in creation. . . . In him we may now penetrate through all the distortion, depravity and degradation of humanity to the true nature of man hidden beneath it all."[191]

Not only is this dynamic conception of truth helpful in explaining creation, fall, and the vicarious humanity of Christ; it is also helpful in explaining the Holy Spirit, because the Spirit of Christ is the Spirit of Truth. Without compromising true human agency, the Spirit acts to clear the confusion between the "already" and the "not yet," who I am in Christ, and who I am in my false Adamic self. In Christ I am my true self, because thanks to him there is no gap between who I am and who I am created to be. In the Spirit, "the being and nature of God [Truth] is brought to bear upon us so that we think under the compulsion of His Reality."[192]

To define true personhood, then, we simply must begin with the person of God, the One who has purposed to bring humanity into a life of mutual love and communion with himself. From an onto-relational perspective we discover that more of grace means *more* of man, not less, and that God is therefore the one "personalizing person." How could the grace of our Lord Jesus Christ, asks TFT, "ever mean a depreciating of the very humanity he came to save?"[193] On the contrary, adds JBT, we are made to share in the Son's personal union with the Father in the Spirit, and "we are never more truly human, never more truly persons, than when we find our true being in communion."[194]

Putting all persons within the realist foundation of Jesus Christ, our truth-keeper, helps us to articulate our theology of sin. To say that

---

190. TFT, *Conflict and Agreement*, 2:70.

191. TFT, "Goodness and Dignity," 315.

192. TFT, *God and Rationality*, 167.

193. TFT, *Mediation of Christ*, xii–xiii.

194. JBT, *Worship, Community*, 62.

Jesus is the truth categorically puts every person in *untruth* and exposes the sinful futility of any attempts to live life "under our own steam." As Paul says in Romans, "Let God be true, and every man a liar" (3:4); humans cannot keep faith with God, no matter how hard we try. Therefore, this hypostatic truth highlights the secondary, or participatory, route of response to God as the only route, and undercuts all co-redemptive attempts. In TFT's manner of speaking, Jesus Christ was the only one who could assume our warped humanity and bend it back, making it straight and true—he who was made perfect through suffering (Heb 2:10).

Finally, in the midst of what seems like the increasing wickedness of the world, inside and outside the church, the truth of God in Christ continues to meet humanity at our hostile worst. Ironically, only Christ can ask our most agnostic and acidic questions in "pure truthfulness." When we hit rock bottom, we are in a position to see Jesus, for Jesus was there first, crying "My God, my God, why hast thou forsaken me?"

> Yet there is hope for man—*in atheism*, if atheism means that his questioning has carried him to the very boundary of creaturely existence, to silence and emptiness and God-forsakenness, to the pure void where man has nothing to say but can only cease and listen. Then it may be that a genuine theology can interpret to him the terrible question of Jesus as the descent of God himself into the dereliction of man in order to take man's atheistical questioning upon his lips, to ask it as we never can in pure truthfulness, and by laying hold of us in our blind hostile questioning in the dark to change it into something that brings light and truth.[195]

Christ's humanity takes him underneath the lowest of the lows, in order to bring humanity to the highest of the highs. In theological persuasion, that is the reality we are calling people to, and that is what we pray by the Spirit of Truth they will see.

> *Send forth your light and your truth, let them guide me;*
> *let them bring me to your holy mountain, to the place where you*
> *dwell.* (Ps 43:3)

---

195. TFT, *Theology in Reconstruction*, 125.

CHAPTER 2
INTRODUCTION

Grace in the Face of Evil

IT IS SWISS DOGMATICIAN Karl Barth who is most recognized as stemming the tide of nineteenth-century German liberalism, preserving the gospel of grace from humanistic influences. Strikingly, Barth and his German friend Dietrich Bonhoeffer tirelessly insisted on the reality of God's redemptive grace in the midst of an era when world war and the Holocaust provided no shortage of evidence to the contrary.

For these men, the person and work of Jesus Christ would not allow for any shades of dualism. In the face of blatant evil and systemic injustice, Barth and Bonhoeffer resisted the temptation to abandon faith and walk by sight. They clung to the biblical and christological truth that everyone is included in the one reality of Christ and that the evil and darkness so prevalent in this world can, no matter how destructive, only be parasitic to that reality; ultimately, there are not two truths, only one truth and the rest counterfeits and distortions. There are not two Kings or two kingdoms, only one King of the kingdom of light opposed by a princely pretender presiding over his God-limited dominion of darkness. There are not two Fathers, only one true Father opposed by an imposter, a deceiver, the father of lies. And finally, ontologically speaking, there are not two categories of people—the children who belong to God and those who do not.

In his watershed reformulation of election, Barth exposed the dualistic nature of Dordtian (Five-Point Calvinism) and Arminian constructs. Barth gave no quarter to the Arminian notion that one crosses over from one truth, that of being unforgiven, unredeemed, separated from God, and Fatherless, to a new truth of being forgiven, redeemed, reconciled, and adopted by God, at the point of decision. Barth knew only too well that our assurance as believers is anchored in what was true about us before we believed it. There is not enough staying power, or assurance, in a relativist dualism that allows me to change the truth about myself with an existential decision.

For Barth and Bonhoeffer, reality is not arbitrary, to be dictated by one's decision; if the truth is not the truth for all, then it's not the truth at all! Of course, in the Dordtian view there is no way to change the truth about oneself with a decision, because in this form of determinist dualism one is locked in for eternity by the decision of God. Consistent with the doctrine of limited atonement, the truth for the minority of humanity is that they are the chosen children of God, whereas the inconvertible truth for the majority is that they are shunned, untouched by Christ's saving work, and damned to hell without a choice. How easy it would be to relegate Hitler and his henchmen to reprobate status, outside the election of God; this is the type of nonchristological theological anthropology that Barth and Bonhoeffer resisted at every turn.

Little did Barth or Bonhoeffer anticipate in 1931 the turbulence that lurked ahead and the effect the Nazi regime would have on their lives. It is not within the purview of this exploration, however, to discuss the immersion of these men in the political mayhem of the period or the extent of their leadership in the Confessing Church. Let it suffice to say that Barth and Bonhoeffer together saw through the evil deceptions of the Third Reich and Hitler's attempts to hijack the church and biblical language to further his anthropocentric and self-serving supremacist agenda. Barth and Bonhoeffer's ethical and political views stemmed consistently from a Christo-realist basis outlined prolifically by Barth in the Barmen Declaration of 1934: "Jesus Christ, as he is attested to us in Holy Scripture, is the one Word of God whom we have to hear, and whom we have to trust and obey in life and in death."

Some of Bonhoeffer's most profound thoughts on grace were penned from his prison cell while he awaited execution for being implicated in a plot against Hitler. The death sentence carried out just before war's end silenced the man but generated great interest in his writings. One of the themes of the ensuing chapter is that Bonhoeffer's famous discussion of "cheap grace" has often been terribly misconstrued by readers who, without their Barthian glasses, have not understood the nature of grace as a double movement. If our conceptualization of grace is not rooted in the incarnation, asserts Bonhoeffer, we will be likely to miss its true meaning. It is only the one-sided, un-incarnational and therefore institutional kind of "grace" that leads to antinomianism and license.

If Barth preserved the gospel from liberalism, he has ironically also been much maligned by the right wing of the church. Barth's refusal to view the doctrine of election as applying only to a subset of the human race, and his exaltation of Christ as the true subject-self of every person, has at times drawn the ire of Dordtians and Arminians alike. To the determinist dualists, who have their own ideas about predestination, Barth is throwing pearls to swine. To the relativistic dualists, who have their own ideas of freedom, Barth is pulling the rug out from under the sacrosanct agency of individuals.

But, as we shall see, Barth's view of election is exhaustively Christ-centered and always interpreted out of God's purposes of grace to choose us all "in the One he loves." Contrary to those who would criticize him for a dominant grace that squelches human response, Barth emphasizes that our proper mode of response in union with Christ is the most personal and free of all. For Barth and Bonhoeffer, obedience motivated by grace is the only true obedience.

The "Yes" of Reality and the Meaning of Grace in Barth and Bonhoeffer

The concept of election means that grace is truly grace.

—KARL BARTH[1]

TOMES HAVE BEEN WRITTEN on the theology of Karl Barth and his student[2] Dietrich Bonhoeffer, and much has been made of the latter's curious "positivism of revelation" charge[3] against his teacher. It will be the aim of this chapter, however, to discuss the impressive similarities

---

1. See Barth, *CD* 2/2:10

2. I use the term *student* loosely but significantly, as undoubtedly Barth was a mentor to the man twenty years his junior. Bonhoeffer biographer Eberhard Bethge prefers to call Bonhoeffer an "ally," not a "pupil," of Barth's (Bethge, *Bonhoeffer*, 141). Alan Torrance has described Bonhoeffer as Barth's "friend and pupil" (A. Torrance, "Trinity," 84), which is certainly the case, despite the fact that Bonhoeffer never officially studied under Barth. Bonhoeffer did visit Barth's seminar in Bonn for three weeks at the end of the summer term, 1931. Here the two men struck up their friendship, and a cordial, honest correspondence ensued. John Phillips goes so far as to say that Bonhoeffer became "personally dependent on the older man" (Phillips, *Form of Christ*, 16).

3. Although there are many theories, no one really knows what Bonhoeffer meant by this charge in the "prison letters" of 1944, which also contain Bonhoeffer's expressions of great respect and admiration for Barth. It appears that some Bonhoeffer scholars in particular want to use "positivism of revelation" to increase the theological separation between Bonhoeffer and the master, as if to bring him out from under Barth's shadow. As Bonhoeffer biographer Eberhard Bethge noted, "When one was tired of Barth, one could go to Bonhoeffer's 'revelation positivism' for one's ammunition" (Bethge, *Bonhoeffer*, 794). Barth himself was confounded over the remark, which he dismissed as one of Bonhoeffer's "enigmatic utterances." Andreas Pangritz offers this explanation: "In his charge of 'positivism of revelation,' Bonhoeffer wanted above all to warn against the danger of saying too much in dogmatics and of becoming 'loquacious'" (Pangritz, *Barth in Bonhoeffer*, 114).

between Barth and Bonhoeffer, exploring especially their Christology, their soteriology, and the inherent interconnections. Moreover, it will be imperative to examine the doctrine of grace so critical to both theologians in an effort to clarify the apparent ambiguity concerning Bonhoeffer's most famous work, *The Cost of Discipleship*. It will be my contention that *The Cost of Discipleship* can be coherently understood only from within a Barthian framework of election.

Dietrich Bonhoeffer was tremendously influenced by Karl Barth's compelling protest against nineteenth-century Protestant liberal theology. As a young divinity student at Berlin University, Bonhoeffer became uneasy with the "anthropological and theological optimism" of Frederick Schleiermacher, Albrecht Ritschl, and others. He "reacted violently against any new attempts to point to a human religious potentiality, no matter how constituted, that led back to investigation of the self."[4] In 1924 Bonhoeffer was introduced to Barth's theology by his cousin, a pupil of Barth's at Gottingen, who gave Bonhoeffer his lecture notes containing the theological underpinnings for Barth's subsequent *Prolegomena to Christian Dogmatics* (1927), a follow-up to his dialectical watershed *Epistle to the Romans* (1919). Bonhoeffer's discovery of Barth's work brought a liberating joy to his own. In place of a restless attempt to focus on the human religious experience, Bonhoeffer found that "the certainty for which he strove was anchored, not in man, but in the majesty of God, with the result that it was not a theme in itself apart from God."[5]

Even as a young Barthian, Bonhoeffer enjoyed testing or critiquing the new theology where he felt Barth was weakest. His allegiance to Barth, however, was unquestionable, and throughout his career he wanted his criticisms to be seen as "coming from inside and not outside the Barthian movement."[6] In fact, notes Clifford Green, "the only theologian to whom [Bonhoeffer] gave real authority in his work" was Karl Barth.[7] When Bonhoeffer crossed the Atlantic in 1930 to spend a year at Union Theological Seminary, the Barthian movement was just reaching American shores. Bonhoeffer proved himself to be a vigorous and capable advocate of Barth in the seminars of John Baillie. Baillie remembers Bonhoeffer as "the most convinced disciple of Dr. Barth that

---

4. Bethge, *Bonhoeffer*, 49.

5. Ibid., 51–52.

6. Ibid., 134.

7. Green, *Bonhoeffer*, 312.

had appeared among us up to that time, and withal as stout an opponent of liberalism as had ever come my way."[8]

In one address delivered at Baillie's seminar, Bonhoeffer began by declaring, "I confess that I do not see any other possible way for you to get into real contact with Barth's thinking than by forgetting, at least for this one hour, everything you have learnt before."[9] Bonhoeffer's brash polemic against liberal theology continued, as he claimed that what was actually fresh in Barth's thought was a return to "the tradition of Paul, Luther, Kierkegaard . . . , the tradition of genuine Christian thinking," a resuscitation of "the world of biblical thinking." Replacing "religious thinking" was the "category of the Word of God . . . , the revelation straight from above, from *outside* of man, according to the justification of the sinner by grace."[10]

Bonhoeffer left Union in 1931 somewhat disillusioned with the theological environment. He recognized his professor of Christian ethics, Reinhold Niebuhr, as "one of the most significant and creative of contemporary American theologians," but he found Niebuhr lacking with regard to "a doctrine of the person and redemptive work of Jesus Christ."[11] "In American theology," Bonhoeffer later noted, "Christianity is essentially religion and ethics. But that means that the person and work of Jesus Christ have to retire into the theological background, and finally remain uncomprehended."[12]

For Bonhoeffer, as for Barth, any discussion of God or ethics that did not start with Jesus Christ was intolerable. T. F. Torrance remarks that for Bonhoeffer, "the point of departure for *Christian ethics* is not the reality of one's own self or the reality of the world, but the reality of God as he reveals himself in Jesus Christ."[13] It is in this connection that we can see

---

8. Cited by Bethge, *Bonhoeffer*, 117.

9. Ibid., 117–18.

10. Cited by Pangritz, *Barth in Bonhoeffer*, 31.

11. Cited by Tinsley, *Bonhoeffer*, 38.

12. Cited by Bethge, *Bonhoeffer*, 564. Indeed, of the ten courses attended by Bonhoeffer at Union, six concerned religion, ethics, and philosophy, including Religion and Ethics, Religious Aspects of Contemporary Philosophy, Ethical Interpretations, Ethical Viewpoints in Modern Literature, and Ethical Issues in the Social Order. There were no courses related to Christology or soteriology.

13. T. F. Torrance, "Cheap and Costly Grace," 305. Torrance continues here: "Bonhoeffer starts, like Barth, from the fundamental principle of justification of the sinner by grace alone which makes a man really free for God and his brothers, for it

not only the strong common ground between Barth and Bonhoeffer, one to which we shall return, but also a helpful differentiation as put forth by Charles Marsh. Marsh notes that while both theologians hold strongly to the one comprehensive reality of God, Barth can be described as emphasizing the primary objectivity (triune life) of God, while Bonhoeffer emphasizes the secondary objectivity (revelation) of God. It is only by the revelation of God that we peer into the triune life, but the triune life is logically primary. "The purpose of this distinction," comments Marsh, "is to stress the priority of God's aseity over his promeity, not in order to forge a dichotomy between God in himself and God in his revelation but simply to say that before all else is, God is God."[14]

The primary and secondary objectivity of God are categories actually first used by Barth himself in *Church Dogmatics* 2/1. There, "Barth states that any compromise of God's trinitarian priority leads to the fateful confusion of God's presence (in the world) and God's identity (in himself), a result of which is the emergence of the notion of general anthropological knowledge of God and a compromise of Christ's uniqueness."[15] Bonhoeffer does not fall prey to this confusion, but his thought can be described, according to Marsh,

> as a continuous wandering along the various paths of the secondary objectivity of revelation, attentive with an intensity not found in Barth to the inner rhythms of worldliness but by no means disregarding the majestic narrative of God's aseity inscribed by him. Bonhoeffer wants to plumb the depths of the meaning of God's promeity; to understand the earth, its riches, delights, and sorrows, in all its christic grandeur. In a sense this is where Bonhoeffer begins and where he ends, in the fascination with the mystery of worldliness, particularly embodied in the mystery of human sociality. His preoccupation with the concreteness of revelation is part and parcel of this fascination.[16]

---

sets his life on a foundation other than himself where he is sustained by a power other than his own."

14. Marsh, *Reclaiming Bonhoeffer*, 31.

15. Ibid., 32.

16. Ibid. It should be noted that for all his emphasis on immanence, Bonhoeffer displays a considerable pneumatological deficiency. Barth is certainly more trinitarian, and even though some have seen a tendency in Barth to conflate the second and third persons of the Trinity, the deficiency is more obvious in Bonhoeffer, for whom "pneumatology is based strictly on christology" (ibid., 74). This weakness is apparent early on in Bonhoeffer's doctoral dissertation, *Sanctorum Communio* (1925): "[The] Holy Spirit

Again, it must be stressed that while perhaps differing in emphasis, Barth and Bonhoeffer alike hold strongly to both the primary and the secondary objectivity of God. Barth does not emphasize aseity at the expense of promeity, or the glory of God at the expense of the humanity of God. Neither does Bonhoeffer focus on the humiliation or promeity of God at the expense of the opposite. Concludes Marsh: "In agreement with Barth, Bonhoeffer holds that the communion of God and humankind is not an anthropological given but is constitutive of God's prior acting in revelation. God alone animates all sacramental encounter. One does not find Christ in the joys and sufferings of the world by virtue of one's own capacity, but only on the basis of the fait accompli of reconciliation."[17] How revelation and reconciliation are united in the person of Jesus Christ is critical for Barth's and Bonhoeffer's understanding of grace, as we shall see.

Bonhoeffer and Barth finally got personally acquainted in 1931, after Bonhoeffer's departure from Union. By that time the qualms the younger theologian had expressed about Barth's theology in *Sanctorum Communio* (1925) and *Act and Being* (1931) had already begun to fall away.[18] Bonhoeffer traveled to Bonn in the summer of 1931, where he spent time with Barth informally and in seminar. In a letter home, Bonhoeffer expressed uncharacteristic fascination with his mentor: "Barth was even better than his books. . . . I was even more impressed by his conversation than by his writings and lectures. In his conversation the whole of him is present. I have not met anything like it before."[19] "I have seldom regretted an omission in my theological past," wrote Bonhoeffer, "so much as not having come [to hear Barth] earlier."[20]

---

has no other content than the fact of Christ" (cited in ibid., 74). It was in the dissertation that he coined the phrase *Christ existing as community*. Bethge asserts that this was Bonhoeffer's reformulation of Hegel's *God existing as community*, which was Hegel's reference to the absolute and pervasive dwelling of the Holy Spirit in the community. Bonhoeffer then "turned the formula into a christological one" (Bethge, *Costly Grace*, 149). If Bonhoeffer's strong Christology was a reaction against Hegel, this may also help to explain his continual subsuming of the Holy Spirit under Christ.

17. Marsh, *Reclaiming Bonhoeffer*, 30.

18. Bethge, *Bonhoeffer*, 137. Of *Sanctorum Communio*, Barth later remarked that it was a "theological miracle" (cited by Godsey, *Bonhoeffer*, 21). Also, in *Church Dogmatics* 4/2, Barth sings the praises of this work by Bonhoeffer (Barth, *CD* 4/2:641).

19. Letter from Bonhoeffer to his parents, cited by Bethge, *Bonhoeffer*, 132.

20. Letter from Bonhoeffer to a friend, cited by Godsey, *Bonhoeffer*, 81.

Barth's progression out of the dialectical period, especially after his study on Anselm (which resulted in his *Anselm* in 1931), and Bonhoeffer's own development reflected in *Act and Being*, brought the two men more to an "eye to eye" theological understanding than ever before.[21] They proceeded into the decade certain that "God's being is in God's becoming for us in Jesus Christ." Continues Marsh:

> This glad news neither denies trinitarian immanence nor sells out to experiential economy; on the contrary, it attests to the equiprimordiality of God's promeity and aseity, or more precisely, to the fact that God's aseity is interpreted by his promeity. "God is not free of man or from humankind, but for humankind" [Bonhoeffer, *Act and Being*]. . . .
>
> . . . In revelation . . . we are not speaking only of an event "which takes place on high, in the mystery of the divine Trinity. . . . But we are now speaking of the revelation of this event on high and therefore our participation in it" [Barth, *CD* 2/1]. We are not speaking of the radical transcendence of dialectical theology but of the God who comes into the world in the self-witness of Jesus Christ. . . . God's acting in Jesus Christ to reconcile the world to himself—to take up humanity into himself—is the act of humanity's salvation.[22]

CHRIST AND THE NEW HUMANITY

We will turn now to our main task of assessing the christological and soteriological thrust of Barth and Bonhoeffer, before noting especially the relationship of election and discipleship in their theologies. It will be necessary to quote Barth and Bonhoeffer often and sometimes at length in order to highlight the convergence of their views regarding the gospel of grace.

> Jesus is *not* the crowning keystone in the arch of *our* thinking. Jesus is *not* a supernatural miracle that we may or may not consider true. Jesus Christ is *not* the goal which we hope to reach after conversion. . . . Jesus Christ is not a figure of our history to which we may "relate" ourselves. And Jesus Christ is *least of all* an object of religion and mystical experience. So far as He is this to us, He is not Jesus Christ. He is God who becomes man, the Creator of all things who lies as a babe in the manger. But as such He is to be

21. Bethge, *Bonhoeffer*, 137.
22. Marsh, *Reclaiming Bonhoeffer*, 13–14, 17.

understood by the other fact that He is the one who was crucified, dead, buried, who descended into hell, but rose again from the dead [Barth, *The Word of God and the Word of Man*].[23]

As already alluded to, it was words like these that signaled the Barthian revolution and caught the attention of the young Dietrich Bonhoeffer. In his University of Berlin Christology lectures of 1933, Bonhoeffer echoes Barth's emphasis on the person of Jesus Christ by homing in on the central issue: not *how* Christ can be both God and man, what Bonhoeffer calls the "alchemy of the incarnation," but *who* this person is who encounters us.[24] We as humans get preoccupied with the *how* question, a question of the fact of revelation that cannot be proven or disproven. Instead, we must move ahead to assess the claim of Christ, the *who* question, "the question of the being, the essence and the nature of Christ. That means that the christological question is fundamentally an ontological question. Its aim is to work out the ontological structure of the 'Who?' without coming to grief on the Scylla of the question 'How?'"[25]

"The only possible meaningful question," asserts Bonhoeffer, "is 'Who is present and contemporaneous with us here?'" In response he is careful, as always, to interpret Christ's being in his act and his act in his being:

> The answer is, "The one person of the God-man Jesus Christ." I do not know who this man Jesus Christ is unless I say at the same time "Jesus Christ is God," and I do not know who the God Jesus Christ is unless I say at the same time "Jesus Christ is man." The two factors cannot be isolated because they are not isolated. God in timeless eternity is not God, Jesus limited by time is not Jesus. Rather, God is God in the man Jesus. In this Jesus Christ God is present. This one God-man is the starting point of christology.[26]

23. Cited in T. F. Torrance, *Karl Barth: Introduction*, 61.

24. Robertson, "Bonhoeffer's Christology," 21. The Christology lectures are not directly from Bonhoeffer's hand but are a compilation of class notes faithfully taken by his students in the summer of 1933. Barth's influence is apparent throughout, although he is not mentioned. In fact, Barth lives "between the lines" of these lectures to such a degree that T. F. Torrance has posited that compiler Eberhard Bethge "systematically suppressed" all references to Barth in the published lectures! Cf. *The Scotsman*, May 28, 1966, and Bethge's sharp rebuttal, June 10, 1966 (Green, *Bonhoeffer*, 206n).

25. Bonhoeffer, *Christology*, 32–33. There are obvious echoes of Kierkegaard here concerning the inadequacy of history or biblical "evidence" to deliver the condition for belief.

26. Ibid., 45–46.

Because of this ontological interpenetration of the two natures in Christ, all humankind is caught up into the humiliation and exaltation of the Incarnate One. "His being Christ is his being *pro me*," that is, his being for me in an ontological way; from this point on, "Christ can never be thought of in his being in himself, but only in his relationship to me."[27] Bonhoeffer pronounces strong judgment against those who have "volatilized" this "being for you" in a fashion that makes Christ's work instrumental only, stripping it of ontological significance and falling back again on the *how*. He writes:

> The decisive element in the *pro me* structure is that the being and action of Christ are maintained within it. . . . The being *for you* and the *being* for you are combined. When the unity of act and being in Jesus Christ is understood in this way, the question of his person, i.e. the question "Who?", can be rightly put.[28]

In binding himself to us and us to himself, concludes Bonhoeffer, Jesus Christ has brothered all of humankind:

> Jesus Christ is for his brethren by standing in their place. Christ stands for his new humanity before God. But if that is the case, he is the new humanity. He stands vicariously where mankind should stand, by virtue of his *pro me* structure. He is the community.[29]

At this stage we must pose the question, Is Bonhoeffer, by putting forth Jesus Christ as the "structure," or form, of the new humanity, in danger of losing the individual humanity of Christ altogether? This question is compounded by statements such as the following found in Bonhoeffer's *Ethics*:

> Jesus is not *a* man. He is *man*. Whatever happens to Him happens to man. It happens to all men, and therefore it happens also to us. The name Jesus contains within itself the whole of humanity and the whole of God.[30]

> Jesus was not the individual, desiring to achieve a perfection of his own, but He lived only as the one who has taken up into Himself and who bears within Himself the selves of all men. All His living, His action and His dying was deputyship.[31]

27. Ibid., 47.
28. Ibid., 48.
29. Ibid., 48–49.
30. Bonhoeffer, *Ethics*, 54.
31. Ibid., 195.

Ernst Feil and Clifford Green are two Bonhoeffer scholars who are keen to interpret the humanity of Christ in social categories. Feil makes much ado about what he calls Bonhoeffer's quiet but significant shift from the *pro me* to the *pro nobis* terminology late in the Christology lectures. This change becomes the basis, according to Feil, for the formulation "Christ—the one for others," found in Bonhoeffer's prison letters. Asserts Feil: "The aspect of sociality comes to full expression only in that change; the vicarious nature of Jesus Christ is itself understood in social categories, for it is not only for me but also for us."[32]

Green insists that "to understand the Christology lectures fully it is necessary to recognize that Bonhoeffer still employs here the concept of the Kollektivperson. As first in *Sanctorum Communio*, so here too, he presents Christ as the Kollektivperson of the new humanity."[33] Still, Green finds himself admitting that in the Christology lectures the term itself does not actually appear.[34] To his credit, Green, as Feil above, recognizes that Bonhoeffer does not exhaustively define Christ's humanity in corporate terms.[35] If there was in the early Bonhoeffer a susceptibility toward diminishing Christ's humanity with the Kollektivperson language, in the Christology lectures there is little evidence of the sort.

In fact, the best evidence that Bonhoeffer holds on to a robust doctrine of the humanity of Christ is found in the Christology lectures themselves. Jesus Christ had to be a real man, asserts Bonhoeffer, because "the real man had to be redeemed."[36] Bonhoeffer inveighs against the litany of heretical Christologies in church history, placing not only Apollinarius but Schleiermacher, Ritschl, and Hegel in the docetist camp. For, notes Bonhoeffer, liberal theology "understands Jesus as the support for or the embodiment of particular ideas, values and doctrines. As a result, the manhood of Christ is in the last resort not taken very seriously, although it is this very theology which speaks so often of the man. . . . It confuses the real man with an ideal man and makes him a symbol."[37]

32. Feil, *Bonhoeffer*, 75.

33. Green, *Bonhoeffer*, 211.

34. Ibid.

35. See ibid., 183: "Christ is interpreted as present in human form in the matrix of social relationships; his presence is the reality of the universal new humanity, in its *corporate and individual dimensions*." Italics mine.

36. Bonhoeffer, *Christology*, 82.

37. Ibid., 83–84.

Most vital in Christology, according to Bonhoeffer, is correct doctrine concerning the sinlessness of Jesus: "It is a central point on which all that has been said is decided." Bonhoeffer frames this critical issue with a series of piercing questions: "Did Jesus, as the humiliated Godman, fully enter into human sin? Was he a man with sins like ours? If not, was he then man at all? If not, can he then help at all? And if he was, how can he help us in our predicament, as he is in the same predicament?" Bonhoeffer cannot and will not go too far in his attempt to resolve the issue of how Christ can assume sinful flesh without sinning. He can only answer the *how* question with both sides of the *who* question:

Christ became involved in the predicament of the whole flesh. But to what extent does he differ from us? In the first place, not at all. . . .

> But everything depends on the fact that it is *he* who took the flesh with its liability to temptation and self-will. . . . Because *he* bears it, this flesh is robbed of its rights. . . . As the one who bears our sin, and no one else, he is sinless, holy, eternal, the Lord, the Son of the Father.[38]

Thus Bonhoeffer finishes the Christology lectures the way he started, with the all-important *who* question. His friend Karl Barth penned it this way: "The ultimate word . . . is not a further thesis, not a synthesis, but just the name Jesus Christ." The two "penultimate words," Barth continued, are "very God and very Man. . . . Our task is to hear the second in the first, the first in the second, and therefore, in a process of thinking and not in a system, to hear the one in both."[39] Bonhoeffer and Barth had great respect for the paradox inherent in the God-man; this translated into a great respect for the mystery of salvation and, especially in Barth, a resistance to systematizing.

For instance, both Barth and Bonhoeffer believed in recapitulation, the Irenaean concept of the re-gathering up of all humanity and the restoration of the world in Jesus Christ. But they also resisted at every point a static triumphalism that depersonalizes humanity or makes belief unnecessary. Remarkably, Bonhoeffer wrote the following during his incarceration:

> Nothing is lost . . . everything is taken up in Christ, although it is transformed, made transparent, clear and free from all selfish desire. Christ restores all this as God originally intended it to be, without the distortion resulting from our sins. The doctrine

38. Ibid., 112–13.
39. Barth, *CD* 1/2:24, 25.

deriving from Eph. 1:10—that of the restoration of all things, *re-capitulatio* (Irenaeus)—is a magnificent conception, full of comfort. This is how the promise "God seeks what has been driven away" is fulfilled.[40]

This same theme is sounded multiple times in *Ethics*: "In Christ 'all things' (Col. 1:17) (i.e., the world [II Cor. 5:19]) are reconciled with God; all things are 'summed up under one head'. . . (Eph. 1:10). Nothing is excepted. In Christ God loved 'the world' (John 3:16)."[41] Bonhoeffer can say, on the one hand, "It is implicit in the New Testament statement concerning the incarnation of God in Christ that all men are taken up, enclosed and borne within the body of Christ,"[42] and yet likewise acknowledge, "It is a mystery, for which there is no explanation, that only a part of mankind recognize the form of their Redeemer. The longing of the Incarnate to take form in all men is as yet still unsatisfied."[43]

Barth too can say that Christ has introduced the eschaton, and that "the recapitulation 'of all things' (1:10) has already taken place in him."[44] At the same time, Barth is keen to adopt recapitulation only as a non-equivalent of universalism:

> It is His concern what is to be the final extent of the circle [of salvation]. If we are to respect the freedom of divine grace, we cannot venture the statement that it must and will finally be coincident with the world of man as such (as in the doctrine of the so-called *apokatastasis*). No such right or necessity can legitimately be deduced.[45]

---

40. Bonhoeffer, *Letters and Papers*, 170. It may be noted that for Bonhoeffer and Barth "being taken up into Christ" does not in any way mean a deification that conflates mankind and God. "The real man is not an object either for contempt or for deification, but an object of the love of God" (Bonhoeffer, *Ethics*, 62).

41. Bonhoeffer, *Ethics*, 288. The brackets are Bonhoeffer's.

42. Ibid., 178. The continuation of this quote reveals Bonhoeffer's theme of "religionless Christianity": "This is just what the congregation of the faithful are to make known to the world by their words and by their lives. What is intended here is not separation from the world but the summoning of the world into the fellowship of this body of Christ, to which in truth it already belongs." Bonhoeffer speaks of the church as an *awakened* subset of the whole of humanity that has been incorporated into the person of Jesus Christ (see ibid., 64–65).

43. Ibid., 63. Recognition comes by the Holy Spirit (see below).

44. Barth, *CD* 4/2:625. I have inserted "recapitulation" for *apokatastasis*, which Barth has written in its Greek form.

45. Barth, *CD* 2/2:417.

Barth cites John 3:16 a few pages later, and for him too "the world" expresses the worldwide scope of God's salvific action. Yet theologians must restrain themselves from attempting to reduce the freedom of the divine love to a system:

> For the fact that Jesus Christ is the reality and revelation of the omnipotent loving-kindness of God towards the whole world and every man is an enduring event which is continually fulfilled in new encounters and transactions, in which God the Father lives and works through the Son, in which the Son of God Himself, and the Holy Spirit of the Father and the Son, lives and works at this or that place or time, in which He rouses and finds faith in this or that man, in which He is recognised and apprehended by this and that man in the promise and in their election—by one here and one there, and therefore by many men! We cannot consider their number as closed, for we can never find any reason for such a limitation in Jesus Christ.... For the very same reason, however, we cannot equate their number with the totality of all men. With the most important of those Johannine texts (3:16), we must be content to say that "God so loved the world, that he gave his only begotten Son, that whosoever believeth in him should not perish, but have everlasting life." This event always concerns those who believe in Him.[46]

Thus it is clear that Bonhoeffer and Barth believed in a world re-created, reconstituted, and reoriented in Jesus Christ.[47] Importantly, it is the Spirit who enables us to believe in Jesus Christ and in what he has already accomplished on our behalf. Only the Spirit can open our eyes to see truth, and until we come to a saving knowledge of this truth, we will live in disorientation. The Holy Spirit will not override our rejection of reality or our stubborn refusal of the One who loves us the most. Barth and Bonhoeffer preached about a God who loves us too much to leave re-orientation to us, and also of a God who loves us too much to force us to live in it.

The new creation and reality itself, then, are comprised in the name of Jesus Christ. In *Creation and Fall* Bonhoeffer writes: "The new is the real end of the old; Christ is the new. Christ is the end of the old. He is not the continuation of the old; he is not its aim, nor is he a consummation upon the line of the old; he is the end and therefore the new."[48] This is

---

46. Ibid., 422.

47. Green, *Bonhoeffer*, 53.

48. Cited in Feil, *Bonhoeffer*, 73.

also a theme prominent in *Ethics*: "The place where the answer is given, both to the question concerning the reality of God and to the question concerning the reality of the world, is designated solely and alone by the name Jesus Christ. . . . In Him all things consist (Col. 1:17). . . . All concepts of reality which do not take account of Him are abstractions."[49] "He is the real one, the origin, essence and goal of all that is real, and for that reason He is Himself the Lord and the Law of the real."[50]

THE INESCAPABLE REALITY

In the lordship of Christ, the law of the real, there is no room for dualism. Barth unequivocally declares:

> We would be ignoring or denying what God has done for us in Jesus Christ if we did not hold steadfastly to the fact that the door has been closed on all dualistic views of evil by the eternal resolve of God which became a historical event on Golgotha, and that not even momentarily can it be opened again. . . . God has broken evil in Jesus Christ, and since he has done this, it is settled once and for all that it can exist only within limits which were fixed beforehand and beyond which it cannot go.[51]

The human cannot, no matter how rebellious, establish an independent existence outside of God's sovereign sphere:

> Not even in hell can he have and enjoy this freedom. Every kind of demon possession is possible, but it is not possible to make the nature and existence of man devilish. Man may fall. Indeed he necessarily falls, and into the abyss, when he sets himself in the wrong against God. But in this fall into the abyss he cannot fall out of the sphere of God and therefore out of the right which God has over him and to him. Even in his most shameful thoughts and words and deeds, even in the most terrible denial and perversion of his good nature, even in the complete forfeiture of his rights and dignity as a man, even in the lowest depths of hell, whatever that may mean for him, he is still the man whom God has elected and created, and as such he is in the hand of God. He has not escaped the right of God over him and to him, but is still subjected to it, utterly and completely. He is still in the sphere of God's jurisdiction.[52]

49. Bonhoeffer, *Ethics*, 167.

50. Ibid., 199–200.

51. Barth, *CD* 4/1:409.

52. Ibid., 534. The idea of "the man whom God has elected" being in hell is not properly understood outside of Barth's doctrine of election discussed below.

Barth wants to explode any myth of an ultimate ontology of sin. Even the fall and its resulting wickedness could not obliterate humans' fundamental ontology, our filial belonging to the God who made us good in God's image and who reconstituted our belonging in the Son. In this context hell has been aptly described as a beating of one's head against the wall of the inescapable reality—the sphere of belongingness.

It is worth noting the great similarity of Bonhoeffer to Barth in this regard:

> We have spoken of reality always in the sense of the reality which is taken up, maintained and reconciled in God. And it is in this sense that we have had to reject all thinking that is conducted in terms of two spheres. . . . The world is not divided between Christ and the devil, but, whether it recognizes it or not, it is solely and entirely the world of Christ. The world is called to this, its reality in Christ. . . . It must be claimed for Him who has won it by His incarnation, His death and His resurrection. Christ gives up nothing of what He has won. He holds it fast in His hands. It is Christ, therefore, who renders inadmissible the dichotomy of a bedevilled and a Christian world. Any static delimitation of a region which belongs to the devil and a region which belongs to Christ is a denial of the reality of God's having reconciled the whole world with Himself in Christ.[53]

It is here where Barth and Bonhoeffer transition from negation of untruth to affirmation of truth; instead of emphasizing the wrongheadedness of thinking in *two* spheres, they exalt the man who has reestablished the *one* in himself: "There is a place at which God and the cosmic reality are reconciled, a place at which God and man have become one. . . . It lies in Jesus Christ, the Reconciler of the world. . . . Behold the man! In Him the world was reconciled with God."[54] There are several passages in *Ethics* where Bonhoeffer seems to be bursting with enthusiasm as he attempts to put the gospel of grace into words. I have selected two, the second of which will provide an ideal jumping-off point for the continuation of this discussion:

> We must leave behind us the picture of the two spheres, and the question now is whether we can replace it with another picture. . . . We shall need above all to direct our gaze to the picture of the

53. Bonhoeffer, *Ethics*, 175–76.
54. Ibid., 8.

body of Christ Himself, who became man, was crucified and rose again. In the body of Jesus Christ God is united with humanity, the whole of humanity is accepted by God, and the world is reconciled with God. In the body of Jesus Christ God took upon himself the sin of the whole world and bore it. There is no part of the world, be it never so forlorn and never so godless, which is not accepted by God and reconciled with God in Jesus Christ. . . . The world belongs to Christ, and it is only in Christ that the world is what it is. It has need, therefore, of nothing less than Christ Himself.[55]

The figure of the Reconciler, of the God-Man Jesus Christ, comes between God and the world and fills the centre of all history. In this figure the secret of the world is laid bare, and in this figure there is revealed the secret of God. No abyss of evil can remain hidden from Him through whom the world is reconciled with God. But the abyss of the love of God encompasses even the most abysmal godlessness of the world. In a manner which passes all comprehension God reverses the judgement of justice and piety, declares Himself guilty towards the world, and thereby wipes out the world's guilt. God Himself sets out on the path of humiliation and atonement, and thereby absolves the world. God is willing to be guilty of our guilt. He takes upon Himself the punishment and the suffering which this guilt has brought on us. God Himself answers for godlessness, love for hatred, the saint for the sinner. Now there is no more godlessness, no more hatred, no more sin which God has not taken upon Himself, suffered for and expiated. Now there is no more reality, no more world, but it is reconciled with God and at peace. God did this in his dear Son Jesus Christ. *Ecce homo!*[56]

Bonhoeffer and Barth want us to know that God's reconciling activity in Christ is much more extensive than simply his "work" on the cross. As we have discussed, Christ's person cannot and must not be separated from his work. If we take the Chalcedonian definition of Jesus Christ seriously, we see that, by virtue of his ontological solidarity with humanity and his eternal solidarity with the Father, when he "grabbed on" to humanity he necessarily sanctified it. In other words, it was not only Christ's substitutionary death that was vicarious but his whole life. As Bonhoeffer is keen to point out, each person is now confronted with "the accomplished reality of the incarnation of God and of the reconcili-

55. Ibid., 177.
56. Ibid., 52.

ation of the world with God in the crib, the cross and the resurrection of Jesus Christ."[57] This is the rich, holistic meaning of the centerpiece statement in the quotation above, "God Himself sets out on the path of humiliation and atonement, and thereby absolves the world."

All of us, in the most real sense possible, have been ontologically woven into the fabric of Christ's humanity. George Hunsinger provides depth to this idea in his book *How to Read Karl Barth*: "The history of every human being is seen [by Barth] as included in that of Jesus. The history of Jesus is taken as the center which establishes, unifies, and incorporates a differentiated whole in which the history of each human being as such is included."[58] When seen in this context, the death of Christ, far from being relegated to the background, becomes the culmination of Christ's struggle against Satan and sinful flesh and the crib-to-cross working out of his perfect sonship. From Calvary we hear the victory cries: "It is finished"; . . . "Father, into your hands I commit my spirit."

In his book on Bonhoeffer, Larry Rasmussen adds:

> The theology of the cross, then, is this: that God happens for us in the humanity of Jesus of Nazareth; that everything we know of God and God's purposes, or of ours and the world's nature and destiny, is buried in the details and drama of that life, death and resurrection; and that Christian faith is a participation in the Being of Jesus, in messianic suffering, where cosmic joy and victory are both hidden and passed along.[59]

All of reality, then, and especially the life of believers (1 Tim 4:10) is bracketed by the grace intrinsic to the person of Jesus Christ; life is about Jesus Christ from beginning to end. As we shall eventually discover, it is this meaning of incarnational grace that Bonhoeffer had in mind when he set out to write *The Cost of Discipleship*.

In Barth's universal application of Colossians 1:13 he employs the brilliant metaphor of "root and soil and country" for the primary, ontological dimension of our grace-full salvation and belonging in Christ:

57. Ibid., 183.

58. Hunsinger, *How to Read Barth*, 108.

59. Rasmussen, *Bonhoeffer*, 155. I have translated "Being of Jesus" from Bonhoeffer's original *Sein Jesu*. Ernst Feil makes reference to Bonhoeffer's dissatisfaction with the Apostles' Creed, which does not convey the nature of Christ's *lifelong* struggle as a man. To the question, "What does 'suffered' signify in the Creed?" Bonhoeffer replied with an answer coinciding with the Heidelberg Catechism: "It sums up the entire life of Jesus Christ" (Feil, *Bonhoeffer*, 71, 216n).

If we are quite clear about His lordship and therefore His love on the one hand, and our own lovelessness and unworthiness of love on the other, it will strike us quite clearly that the autonomy of our existence has been taken from us. He has taken it to Himself; He has not taken away our existence from us. We have not ceased to be ourselves. We are still free. But in that existence He has left us without root or soil or country, "having transferred us to the Kingdom of the Son of his love" (Col. 1:13), having Himself become our root and soil and country. From the standpoint of His incarnation and exaltation, the fact that we are "translated into the kingdom of the Son of God" means that as the Second Adam He has assumed human nature, that He has united it to His divine person, so that our humanity, our existence in this nature, no longer has any particularity of its own, but belongs only to Him. And from the standpoint of the reconciliation and justification effected in Him, it means that, bearing our punishment, achieving the obedience we did not achieve and keeping the faith we did not keep, He acted once and for all in our place. We cannot, therefore, seek our own being and activity, so far as they still remain to us, in ourselves but only in Him. . . . This being and activity acquires a direction at the point where everything is done for us, the direction Godward in Jesus Christ.[60]

To this point we may summarize our study of the Christology of Barth and Bonhoeffer by saying that God's whole relationship with humanity happens in the person of Jesus Christ, the reconciler of the world. As the Second Adam, Jesus Christ's life, death, resurrection, and ascension have universal application. All the while the Holy Spirit, without violating our God-given freedom and our created dignity, seeks to draw men and women into belief so that they may bask in God's love and thankfully marvel at what Christ has done and is doing on their behalf.

It is worth emphasizing here the dynamic nature of what Barth above calls the "direction Godward" of human life. Too often Barth has been misunderstood as describing the triumph of grace as a one-way movement, as if the direction of grace were only from God to humanity. Perhaps this is because we have a tendency to objectify God and think of Christ doing something for us "over there," as if we humans were standing "over here" as spectators, assessing his work and contemplating or even appreciating the benefits he provides for us in a way that is external

---

60. Barth, *CD* 1/2:391–92.

to us. We easily forget that when Christ does something for us, it is really vicariously for each of us, in our place, from our side, from our shoes.

If we miss the reciprocal aspect of grace, we stand to lose theological footing in critical areas, including the atonement, election, and ethics: without the ontology intrinsic to the incarnational union of Christ with every human being, the atonement, even if it maintains its substitutionary basis, is evacuated of its representative character and thereby becomes increasingly limited and forensic; universal election collapses into universalism, because, without the freedom to choose the one who has chosen us, human agency is compromised; and cheap grace ruins any chance of a Christo-centric ethic, for which legalism and license, ironically both symptomatic of this wreckage, are destructive substitutes.

That is why, for Barth and Bonhoeffer, the word *mediator* is freighted with meaning: "For there is one God and one mediator between God and men, the man Christ Jesus, who gave himself as a ransom for all men" (1 Tim 2:5–6). For these theologians, God's sovereignty *over* all is consistently coupled with God's solidarity *with* us all. God the Son, our human brother and mediator Jesus Christ, represents God to us and us to God; he is in his person the God-humanward movement and the human-Godward movement of salvation history. Here we are reminded that as the one true human (and inside that, as the one true Israelite), Christ keeps the covenant from both sides! Barth expounds on Christ's unique ability to minister the things of God to humans and the things of humans to God:

> In the word of the Gospel Christ takes our place, *really* undertaking and conducting God's case with us and our case with God. It was His conducting of God's case with us sinners that brought Him to the cross, and His conducting of our sinners' case with God is the eternal effect, the victorious result of His suffering and death. If it is true that this did happen and was consummated through Him who could actually do it, if it is true that as true God and true man He intercedes for God with us and for us with God, then we are in fact no longer the object of the divine accusation and threat. It is then the burden which is taken from us by God Himself and is laid entirely upon Christ. But for us remains life in a freedom for which we have to thank the compassion that became event in Christ.[61]

61. Ibid., 113. Italics mine.

I have highlighted *really* above to emphasize Barth's point that if Christ had not become fully human, assuming human flesh, he could not be our mediator in the truest sense of the word. Instead, he would be some kind of pre-fall human functionary who acts to intervene between two other parties. His role would be to pacify God and assuage God's wrath toward humanity. He would not, in this scenario, *really* stand in our place; he would not *really* be in solidarity, *homoousios*, with us. Instead of something that happens internal to his person, reconciliation would be external to him. To use our earlier language, the cross would then stress the act of God in Christ, but not his being; without Christ being *homoousios* with God and *homoousios* with humanity, the onto-logical significance of the incarnation would disappear.

This critical discussion of Christ's mediatorship is handled superbly by Heinrich Ott in his work *Reality and Faith: The Theological Legacy of Dietrich Bonhoeffer*. First Ott describes the external, or instrumental, view of the atonement:

> The Mediator enters into this moralist and juridical relation, pays the debt, and thus restores the relation again. . . . Connected with this, while the Mediator is indeed a person, as he has to be, he is not as Mediator interesting and relevant because of himself, because of the person he is, but only by virtue of his position as Mediator in the moralist and juridical relation between two other persons. The "substance" of his being as Mediator thus in a certain sense exhausts itself in this relation.[62]

In contrast, Ott then articulates the internal, or ontological, view, one in which we observe in Christ the beautiful coinherence of the act of God in his being and the being of God in his act:

> The truth is given by John 14:6, "I am the way, the truth and the life. No man cometh to the Father but by me." This is the being of the Mediator, he is truth itself and life itself. The Giver of the gift of God is himself the gift. The Revealer of the Word of God is himself the Word which he speaks. He is the reality in which we live, in which we have found ourselves since our birth, the reality that God looks graciously upon us and upon all his creatures. . . . So understood, the Mediator is not merely someone who takes his part in the play, even if it were the most important part of all. One might say that he himself is the stage on which we all play the parts of our life before the face of God.[63]

62. Ott, *Reality and Faith*, 390.
63. Ibid., 393.

"On stage" may not be the best equivalent for "in Christ," but it helps expose the problem with the instrumental view as Bonhoeffer and Barth saw it.

Clearly, Barth and Bonhoeffer saw that incarnation cannot be separated from atonement any more than one can separate the two natures of Jesus Christ. It should be obvious by now how much the Torrances' view concerning this "divine-human reality" (outlined in chapter 1) is influenced by their mentor. T. F. Torrance remembers how, for Barth, "the ontological and the dynamic, the Christological and the soteriological, were never held apart but were allowed to come to expression as the two sides of the great truth of the Gospel."[64]

Barth was, continues Torrance, vehemently opposed to the belief that "in the atonement Christ could be thought of as assuming our actual sin, but not our original sin, and then only by some external moral or forensic transaction."[65] This idea "that the Son of God took some kind of neutral human nature upon himself . . . was evangelically and soteriologically deficient" to Barth, "for it drove a damaging wedge between incarnation and atonement and separated being from activity in the incarnate Person of the Mediator."[66]

Torrance concludes: "As Barth taught, reiterating John Calvin, from the very moment of his birth when Jesus put on the form of a servant, he was at work redeeming human nature."[67]

> All this means that incarnation and atonement are entwined in one another from the very birth of Jesus and operate unceasingly together as they press toward the climactic accomplishment of his vicarious ministry of reconciliation and redemption in his propitiatory and substitutionary death and resurrection. In the centre of it all is the Person of Jesus Christ, the Mediator, God with us in such a way that in him we are with God. In the deepest sense Jesus Christ is himself the atonement.[68]

For Barth and Bonhoeffer, Jesus Christ *is* life, Jesus Christ *is* grace; he is the reality of reconciliation, justification, redemption, salvation, and

---

64. T. F. Torrance, *Karl Barth: Theologian*, 178.

65. Ibid., 202. Torrance here notes Barth's firm footing in the tradition of the patristics, adhering to their guiding doctrine that "the unassumed is the unhealed."

66. Ibid., 179.

67. Ibid.

68. Ibid., 204.

atonement in his person. This is a reality in which every human being is unavoidably involved.

THE DYNAMIC NATURE OF ELECTION

This context naturally extends us into a brief discussion of Barth's breathtaking doctrine of election, the revolutionary biblical insight that Jesus Christ "is the Elect of God,"[69] which had such a profound impact on Bonhoeffer.

It should come as no surprise that for Barth, Jesus Christ is both elector and elected, the subject and object of election. Every human being has truly been justified by grace, and any subjective response we may make to God can only be understood against the backdrop of the prior and primary response Christ made to the Father on our behalf. "He did what he has done in our place, for us," says Barth, "so the answer which God the Father gave Him in respect of His act of obedience applies to us."[70] Jesus Christ our brother and Savior has put our name on his answer![71]

T. F. Torrance adds: "That is why justification remains the most powerful statement of objectivity in theology, for it throws us at every point upon the Reality of God and what He has done for us in Christ, and will never let us rest upon our own efforts."[72] Left alone to our own devices, we in our sinful condition are hopeless, mired in unrighteousness. In our rebellion we have said "no" to God. Yet in his great mercy and love, God has said "Yes" to us in Jesus Christ, God's Elected One. In Christ, God exercises God's prerogative: the right of a righteous God to make things right. The justification of human beings by God, declares Barth, is done "in harmony with Himself," for "He is just in Himself." Therefore, his election in Christ is not an unreliable "Yes" and "No" but the plain "Yes" of God (2 Cor 1:19).[73]

69. Barth, *CD* 2/2:740.

70. Barth, *CD* 4/1:556–57.

71. I owe this comment to my friend Dr. C. Baxter Kruger, who studied under J. B. Torrance at Aberdeen. Kruger has published many helpful books in the vein of our study, and his Perichoresis.org offers a wealth of resources.

72. T. F. Torrance, "Cheap and Costly Grace," 299.

73. Barth, *CD* 4/1:529–31.

God does not owe grace to his creatures. The undeserved nature of God's free election of humanity in Christ comes crashing through in this passage of *Church Dogmatics*:

> Grace is the Nevertheless of the divine love to the creature. The election consists in this Nevertheless. It is indeed election. It is indeed grace, and for that reason it is free. How could the divine love to the creature be really love, how could it be divine, unless it were free? But it is grace, loving-kindness, favour. In it God says Yes to the creature and not No. He says it of Himself. He says it without the creature having any right or claim to it. He says it then, in freedom. . . . He does not say No but Yes. Against our No He places His own Nevertheless. He is free in the very fact that the creature's opposition to His love cannot be any obstacle to Him. . . . He is free . . . in the fact that He can rescue the creature from the destruction into which it has plunged itself by its opposition. He is free in the fact that He can turn it in spite of itself to the salvation and life which are the positive and the distinctive meaning and goal of His love. And it is that which God elects. It is that which He does in the election of His grace. He chooses the Yes and not the No, inevitable as the latter seems in face of the attitude of the creature.[74]

This divine "Yes" is as unconditional and unlimited as it is undeserved, as Barth powerfully proclaims to the inmates of Basel Prison:

> He is not against us; he is for us. This is God's mercy. Contrary to human mercy in even its kindest expression, God's mercy is almighty. . . . We need not be afraid that it might be limited or have strings attached. His "yes" is unequivocal, never to be reversed into "no."[75]

Significantly, and this is a point on which Barth is often misunderstood, God does not say "Yes" to our "no." To do so would entail a tolerance of evil and rebellion that, far from putting things right, would be an acceptance of wrong. In fact, the "Yes" of God is not spoken first and foremost to us at all, but to the Elected One, the Man who as our mediator has said "Yes" for us on our behalf. The inner meaning of the eternal covenant of grace, then, is humanity's inclusion in the "Yes" that is really a double "Yes." The "Yes" of election means that God has said "Yes" to us and "Yes" for us in Jesus Christ. Grace is a "Yes" to a "Yes"!

74. Ibid., 2/2:28–29.
75. Barth, "All," 87. The sermon was delivered September 22, 1957.

We must understand ourselves to be elect only via incorporation into the life of the Elected One. In other words, the "Yes" of God on behalf of human beings must also be seen as an indictment against our sinful selves in our inability to say our own "yes" to God. In this triumphant "Yes," therefore, is couched a severe "No" to our reprobate existence. Relates Barth:

> It is because and as God issues the command to proceed that He also issues the command to halt, and not conversely. He kills the old man by introducing the new, and not conversely. It is with His Yes to the man elected and loved and called by Him that He says No to his sinful existence, forcing him to recognize that we are always in the wrong before God.[76]

Because we can only say "no" to God, Jesus Christ chooses to substitute for us all and supply his representative "Yes." Amazingly, he not only chooses to represent us with his "Yes," he also chooses to represent our "no" and thereby to absorb the divine "No" directed to our old existence. It is because God says "Yes" to our "Yes" in Christ that God says "No" to our "no." Here we see, acknowledges Barth, that God's "wrath is the burning of His love," and that "divine wrath does not really exist apart from grace."[77]

The "Yes" is not hidden in the "No" but vice versa; God's judgment, then, serves his love. "Genuine wrath is obviously possible only on the basis and in the context of original and true love,"[78] as Barth continues to express:

> God judges us . . . because He has given us everything in His Son Jesus Christ. . . . It is in Him that He judges us. . . . In Jesus Christ He has chosen man from all eternity as His own, for life in His kingdom, to be a member of His people, His possession. . . . In Him He has loved us, and we are those who are loved by Him. . . . The love of God is the real presupposition of the divine judgment.[79]

In excerpts from another sermon at Basel, Barth colorfully expounds on the great truth of the Judge being judged in our place:

---

76. Barth, *CD* 4/2:577.
77. Ibid., 2/2:720, 721.
78. Ibid., 735.
79. Ibid., 736–37.

The death of Jesus was a *judgment*. . . . God has spoken his "No" to the whole inventory of the old man in us, having no use for him, discarding him, delivering him to death. What Jesus had to bear in our place was nothing less than this hard and irrevocable "No," spoken by God upon this old man in us. Jesus accepted to die the death of the old man. He suffered this death in his flesh.

> . . . That he may himself say to us his divine "Yes" valid once for all and unconditionally, he has chosen to say his divine "No," once for all and unconditionally, to this old companion who has no traffic with our true self.[80]

We have observed how God became the subject and object of God's election, and how the divine "Yes" and "No" took place in the person of Christ himself. Jesus Christ is the Elected One and the Rejected One, our justification and contradiction, and hidden in the sphere of the divine "Yes" is the divine "No." It is only in light of the "Yes" that we can understand the "No." Barth's words above bear repeating: "because He has given us everything in His Son Jesus Christ" [the "Yes"], "God judges us" [the "No"].

It is within Barth's doctrine of election that we see the proper place for all talk of justification. Justification has nothing to do with an external pardon of sin or with an accommodation of the sinner; our righteous and holy God would not be satisfied until the rebellious human "no" was destroyed and subsequently converted into a righteous human "Yes." The justification of the wicked happened once and for all when we died and rose in the person of our Savior. In the crucifixion of the old humanity and the resurrection of the new, humankind has been translated from the history of Adam to the future of Jesus (Rom 5:18). And in the divine "No" and in the divine "Yes" we hear one thing loud and clear: God is for us!

With Barth, Dietrich Bonhoeffer believed that "the doctrine of the divine election of grace is the sum of the Gospel."[81] He writes in *Ethics*: "Jesus Christ is not the transfiguration of sublime humanity. He is the 'yes' which God addresses to the real man . . . the merciful 'yes' of Him

---

80. Barth, "Teach Us," 121–22, 123. Delivered March 16, 1958. I have taken the liberty of capitalizing "Yes" and "No" in order to maintain consistency.

81. Barth, *CD* 2/2:10.

who has compassion. In this 'yes' there is comprised the whole life and the whole hope of the world."[82] With forceful flair Bonhoeffer adds:

> *Ecce homo!*—Behold the man who has been taken to Himself by God, sentenced and executed and awakened by God to a new life. Behold the Risen One. The "yes" which God addresses to man has achieved its purpose through and beyond judgement and death. God's love for man has proved stronger than death. By God's miracle there has been created a new man, a new life, a new creature. "Life has secured the victory. It has overcome death." God's love has become the death of death and the life of man. Humanity has been made new in Jesus Christ, who became man, was crucified and rose again. What befell Christ befell all men, for Christ was man. The new man has been created.[83]

Christ indeed suffers "the curse of the divine 'no,'" but "in bringing us death this 'no' becomes a mysterious 'yes,' the affirmation of a new life, the life which is Jesus Christ."[84] In one of his most important statements regarding grace in all of *Ethics*, Bonhoeffer continues with his definition of this "life which is Jesus Christ":

> It is the "yes" of creation, atonement and redemption, and the "no" of the condemnation and death of the life which has fallen away from its origin, its essence and its goal. But no one who knows Christ can hear the "yes" without the "no" or the "no" without the "yes." . . . If that were so, the "yes" and the "no" would lose their unity in Jesus Christ, but this new life is one in Jesus Christ; it is in tension between the "yes" and the "no" in the sense that in every "yes" the "no" is already heard and in every "no" there is heard also the "yes."[85]

Like incarnation and atonement, revelation and reconciliation, and Christology and soteriology, for Barth and Bonhoeffer the "Yes" and the "No" cannot be separated. To know Jesus Christ is to know God's "kind severity" and "severe kindness" all at once. To appreciate grace is to hear the "No" in the "Yes"; it is to understand that grace is God's "Yes" to our "Yes," our "Yes" that simply cannot be uttered by us at all, but was freely

---

82. Bonhoeffer, *Ethics*, 53.

83. Ibid., 59.

84. Ibid., 199, 189.

85. Ibid., 190. Cf. *CD* 4/1:591: "As His affirmation of sinful man it includes his negation. The Yes cannot be heard unless the No is also heard."

spoken for us by our Lord Jesus Christ and provided *in* his very person. It is this meaning of grace, what we shall call "incarnational grace," that provided the foundation upon which Bonhoeffer was to write *The Cost of Discipleship.* And, as we shall see, only a Christo-realist foundation can protect us from legalism on one side and license on the other.

INCARNATIONAL GRACE AND OBEDIENCE

The Cost of Discipleship is a polemical work concerning what Bonhoeffer sees as an abusive misunderstanding of grace in the church. In chapter 1, "Costly Grace," Bonhoeffer asserts: "Cheap grace means the justification of sin without the justification of the sinner. Grace alone does everything, they say, and so everything can remain as it was before." This attitude, he says, provides a "cheap covering" for sins; "no contrition is required, still less any real desire to be delivered from sin."[86] Bonhoeffer continues: "It is under the influence of this kind of 'grace' that the world has been made 'Christian,' but at the cost of secularizing the Christian religion as never before. . . . I need no longer try to follow Christ, for cheap grace, the bitterest foe of discipleship, . . . has freed me from that."[87] Further on in chapter 1, Bonhoeffer presses his attack:

> This cheap grace has been no less disastrous to our own spiritual lives. Instead of opening up the way to Christ it has closed it. Instead of calling us to follow Christ, it has hardened us in our disobedience. Perhaps we had once heard the gracious call to follow him, and had at this command even taken the first few steps along the path of discipleship in the discipline of obedience, only to find ourselves confronted by the word of cheap grace. . . . The only effect that such a word could have on us was to bar our way to progress, and seduce us to the mediocre level of the world . . . , telling us . . . that we were spending our strength and disciplining ourselves in vain—all of which was not merely useless, but extremely dangerous. After all, we were told, our salvation had already been accomplished by the grace of God. . . . The word of cheap grace has been the ruin of more Christians than any commandment of works.[88]

---

86. Bonhoeffer, *Cost of Discipleship*, 35.

87. Ibid., 42.

88. Ibid., 46.

Is this the same Bonhoeffer we have grown accustomed to thus far in our study? Our Barthian champion of unconditional grace? How do we make sense of demanding statements like "only he who believes is obedient, and only he who is obedient believes,"[89] or in his chapter "Discipleship and the Cross" the remark, "When Christ calls a man, he bids him come and die"?[90] After the first few chapters Bonhoeffer begins an extended exegesis of the Sermon on the Mount and finishes the book with a discussion of various topics related to discipleship. These sections are replete with directives to deny self, slough off lethargy, and abjectly obey the Lord. There is little room for failure[91] or hesitation:

> Humanly speaking, we could understand and interpret the Sermon on the Mount in a thousand different ways. Jesus knows only one possibility: simple surrender and obedience, not interpreting it or applying it, but doing and obeying it. That is the only way to hear his word. But again he does not mean that it is to be discussed as an ideal, he really means us to get on with it.[92]

Clifford Green is one who has taken *The Cost of Discipleship* as a bugle call to fall in march behind the Commander.[93] He notes Bonhoeffer's disgruntlement with lip-service Christianity and believes "the predominant strain in the Christology of *Discipleship* is the power and authority of Christ."[94] Green adds: "Jesus Christ is the one 'absolute authority' over and above all human authorities; discipleship is simple, unreflective faith, and faith is genuine only in discipleship, i.e., *following*—simple

---

89. Ibid., 54.

90. Ibid., 79.

91. See ibid., 116: "Jesus will not accept the common distinction between righteous indignation and unjustifiable anger. The disciple must be entirely innocent of anger, because anger is an offence against both God and his neighbour. . . . When a man gets angry with his brother and swears at him, when he publicly insults or slanders him, he is guilty of murder and forfeits his relationship to God. . . . If we despise our brother our worship is unreal, and it forfeits every divine promise."

92. Ibid., 175.

93. Green is certainly not alone, as *The Cost of Discipleship* is still being interpreted and even sold as a sort of "pep talk" for the unmotivated Christian: "This book will challenge you to shake off all complacency and start taking up the cross to follow Christ" (Amazon.co.uk website, Feb. 6, 2000).

94. Green, *Bonhoeffer*, 138.

obedience to the commandment of Christ."[95] Essentially, true disciple-ship entails a power struggle:

> Obedience was Bonhoeffer's answer to the powerful, ambitious, successful, self-confident, autonomous ego. Here is the heart of the matter. If the ego is living by its own autonomous power, that power must be overcome and made obedient to the authority of Christ. . . . The disciple must make a complete *break* [Bruch] with his former way of life, and this involves the complete surrender, mortification and renunciation of his own will. Bonhoeffer, to be sure, speaks of the grace, love, and forgiveness of Christ, and of the disciple being justified by faith; he speaks, too, of the joy, confidence, and freedom of the disciple. But these are set strictly within the context of the authority of Christ's commands and the obedience these demand. In short, the theology of *Discipleship* presents Christ as a mighty power who defeats the strong self-will of the powerful, autonomous human ego.[96]

We must seriously question Green's thesis, for it lends itself to the muscular Christianity Bonhoeffer wanted so much to avoid, putting grace in the context of law instead of the other way around. That is certainly not what Bonhoeffer set out to communicate in *The Cost of Discipleship*. One has to wonder how seriously Green has considered Bonhoeffer's Barthian perspective, much less Bonhoeffer's introduction to *The Cost of Discipleship*, where he clearly delineates the book's purpose. Green asks and answers, "How does one move from the phraseological to the reality of faith? . . . Bonhoeffer's answer is categorical: obedience."[97] I disagree; Bonhoeffer's answer is grace. Green asserts that for Bonhoeffer, "the understanding of law and gospel which offers grace without requir-ing obedience offers 'cheap grace.'"[98] I counter that grace contingent on obedience is no grace at all. A Barthian reading of the text makes much better sense of Bonhoeffer's arguments in the first section of the book.

In the introduction to *The Cost of Discipleship* it is obvious that for Bonhoeffer, grace is about God's unconditional "Yes" in the person of Jesus Christ. His call for us to be committed to him is wrapped up in his commitment to us. All of our striving is within the context of our belonging, reminiscent of Paul's comment, "I press on to make it my

95. Ibid., 151–52.

96. Ibid., 162.

97. Ibid., 160.

98. Ibid., 152.

own because Christ Jesus has made me his own." Contrary to the stern language of Green, when Christ calls a person to obey it means taking off the heavy yoke and putting on the light one. Discipleship is not about a power struggle, but about a love relationship. Indeed, Christ stands against autonomous persons, but that is because he has already stood in the place of every person:

> If Christianity means following Christ, is it not a religion for a small minority, a spiritual elite? Does it not mean the repudiation of the great mass of society, and a hearty contempt for the weak and the poor? Yet surely such an attitude is the exact opposite of the gracious mercy of Jesus Christ, who came to the publicans and sinners, the weak and the poor, the erring and the hopeless. Are those who belong to Jesus only a few, or are they many? . . . With him were crucified, not two of his followers, but two murderers. But they all stood beneath the cross, enemies and believers, doubters and cowards, revilers and devoted followers. His prayer, in that hour, and his forgiveness, was meant for them all, and for all their sins. The mercy and love of God are at work even in the midst of his enemies. It is the same Jesus Christ, who of his grace calls us to follow him.[99]

For Bonhoeffer, the motivation to follow and the empowerment to obey derive from the joy of grace; abject obedience reliant on willpower produces "martyrs," not disciples. Bonhoeffer knew the secret, that grace "teaches us to say 'No' to ungodliness" (Titus 2:12).

Yet even as I disagree with Green, I must acknowledge that he read the same *Cost of Discipleship* that I did! In other words, Bonhoeffer does diverge from his emphasis on unconditional grace (a fact he later regretted), and there is plenty of substantiation for Green's commandment-driven thesis in the middle and latter portions of the book.

Grace is free, but because it seems loose and reckless, we often feel a responsibility to tighten it up. Out of fear of promoting a license to sin we want to make grace conditional, to prop it up by emphasizing the imperatives of law over the indicatives of grace. We have noted my friend J. B. Torrance's assertion that the great sin of the human heart is to turn God's covenant into a contract. Bonhoeffer seems to succumb to this tendency

---

99. Bonhoeffer, *Cost of Discipleship*, 31–32. For an enlightened discussion of Christ standing against us in the very best sense, see Bonhoeffer's theology of the "Anti-Logos" in *Christology*, 29–37.

in parts of *The Cost of Discipleship*, perhaps in frustration over abuses in the church, which caused him to overreact and to constrict his definitions of grace and the body of Christ in the world. I take that to be Bonhoeffer's meaning in a letter he wrote from prison in 1943: "I thought I could acquire faith by trying to live a holy life, or something like it. I suppose I wrote *The Cost of Discipleship* as the end of that path. Today I can see the dangers of that book, though I still stand by what I wrote."[100]

But, again, we must refuse to categorize the book in Green's fashion, for *The Cost of Discipleship* is sprinkled with gems of grace, and to overlook the first five chapters would be to miss one of the finest Barthian expositions of grace ever penned. Barth himself gives a glowing tribute to Bonhoeffer at the beginning of his section "The Call to Discipleship" in *Church Dogmatics*:

> Easily the best that has been written on this subject is to be found in *The Cost of Discipleship*, by Dietrich Bonhoeffer. . . . We do not refer to all the parts, which were obviously compiled from different sources, but to the opening sections. . . . In these the matter is handled with such depth and precision that I am almost tempted simply to reproduce them in an extended quotation. For I cannot hope to say anything better on the subject than what is said here by a man who, having written on discipleship, was ready to achieve it in his own life, and did in his own way achieve it even to the point of death. In following my own course, I am happy that on this occasion I can lean as heavily as I do upon another.[101]

It is now time to elaborate on the proper connection between grace and obedience in *The Cost of Discipleship*. We must not let Bonhoeffer's polemic against "cheap grace" convolute the meaning of grace. As L. Gregory Jones has pointed out, we must begin by recognizing that the expression "cheap grace" is itself an oxymoron.[102] Grace is free and

100. Bonhoeffer, *Letters and Papers*, 369. Ray Anderson substantiates my surmise: "I agree that in COD Bonhoeffer was following Barth's 'unconditional grace' as the underlying assumption so that the indicative . . . can then lead to the imperative—unconditional obedience. . . . What D. B. might have seen in the 'danger' of COD is that it makes the imperative precede the indicative so that 'costly grace' becomes a 'method' to gain righteousness rather than a gracious freedom to follow Christ" (personal correspondence, March 14, 2002).

101. Barth, *CD* 4/2:533. While I believe that the key to the book is found in these early chapters, I am also wary of lopping off the second half of *The Cost of Discipleship* and disregarding it as useless. Bonhoeffer has some fine moments throughout.

102. Jones, *Embodying Forgiveness*, 159.

therefore cannot be "cheap." What then does Bonhoeffer mean by the term? In his words: "Cheap grace means grace as a doctrine, a principle, a system. It means forgiveness of sins proclaimed as a general truth."[103] Furthermore, "it means that I can set out to live the Christian life in the world with all my sins justified beforehand. I can go and sin as much as I like, and rely on this grace to forgive me, for after all the world is justified in principle by grace."[104]

Has our salvation been accomplished by the grace of God? NO! This is the critical point. The world's salvation and justification has not been accomplished by a *principle*, but by a *person*. "Cheap grace," remarks Bonhoeffer, "is a denial of the Incarnation of the Word of God."[105] A subtle and disastrous shift takes place when grace becomes impersonal and when it is disconnected from Jesus, *in* whom our salvation literally took place; the programming of grace ironically and noxiously morphs into a legalism of grace![106] Grace cannot be reduced to an extra-Christic commodity or soteriological salve. The Gift cannot be divorced from the Giver. For Bonhoeffer, as we have seen all along, the incarnation is atonement, revelation is reconciliation, Christology is soteriology. Jesus Christ is saving grace in his person.

Even in *The Cost of Discipleship* Bonhoeffer connects incarnation and atonement in Christ. These are the truths on which Bonhoeffer based all Christian discipleship and ethics:

> The Body of Jesus Christ, in which we are taken up with the whole human race, has now become the ground of our salvation.
>
> It is *sinful* flesh that he bears, though he was himself without sin. . . . In his human body he takes all flesh upon himself. . . . .
>
> Consequently the incarnate Son of God existed so to speak in two capacities—in his own person, and as the representative of the new humanity. Every act he wrought was performed on behalf of the new humanity which he bore in his body. . . .
>
> . . . All whom he bore suffer and die with him. It is all our infirmities and all our sin that he bears at the cross. It is *we* who are crucified with him, and we who die with him. . . . And so as he dies, Jesus bears the human race, and carries it onward to

---

103. Bonhoeffer, *Cost of Discipleship*, 35.
104. Ibid., 42.
105. Ibid., 35.
106. Ibid., 87.

resurrection. Thus, too, he bears for ever in his glorified body the humanity which he had taken upon him on earth. . . .

All men are "with Christ" as a consequence of the Incarnation, for in the Incarnation Jesus bore our whole human nature. That is why his life, death and resurrection are events which involve all men. . . . But Christians are "with Christ" in a special sense.[107]

Unfortunately, these passages are buried in the later part of the book, too late to help most readers make sense of Bonhoeffer's statement in chapter 1 that "cheap grace is a denial of the Incarnation of the Word of God." If we do not mentally unpack this comprehensive word "Incarnation" while reading *The Cost of Discipleship*, we will think Bonhoeffer is trying to condition grace when he calls for "costly grace."

"Costly grace," then, is mediated grace. Simply put by Bonhoeffer, "Costly grace is the Incarnation of God." This is opposed to "cheap grace," defined as "grace without Jesus Christ, living and incarnate."[108] Asserts Bonhoeffer: "Because the Son of God became Man, . . . the only true relation we can have with him is to follow him. Discipleship is bound to Christ as the Mediator, and where it is properly understood, it necessarily implies faith in the Son of God as the Mediator. Only the Mediator, the God-man, can call men to follow him."[109] Cheap grace is unmediated; it is "the grace we bestow on ourselves," says Bonhoeffer.[110] It leaves out Jesus Christ altogether, and in doing so disconnects us from ontological involvement with his person and work. Grace that is not incarnational is simply mythological.

Grace pure and simple is God's unconditional "Yes" to our "Yes," provided only in Jesus Christ, the Elected One in whom the world is elected. "Cheap grace" would be God's "Yes" to our "no." It would mean God saying "Yes" to our sins, instead of "Yes" to us as sinners in spite of our sins. Hence, cheap grace is not grace at all, for grace is inherently costly.

---

107. Ibid., 213, 214, 215. In the final paragraph here, Bonhoeffer cites Rom 5:18ff; 1 Cor 15:22; and 2 Cor 5:14. As for being "with Christ" in a special sense, this comes by the Holy Spirit, who brings *metanoia*, an awakening to belief in Christ and thankful acknowledgment for what he has accomplished on our behalf.

108. Ibid., 36–37.

109. Ibid., 50. Notes Feil regarding *The Cost of Discipleship*: "Nowhere else in Bonhoeffer's work is Christ referred to as mediator with such force" (Feil, *Bonhoeffer*, 79).

110. Bonhoeffer, *Cost of Discipleship*, 36.

Grace is costly because it includes hidden within it the divine "No," the shedding of the blood of the Son of God. Out of his boundless love, the reconciler of humankind executed judgment upon himself; "this is the great price which God pays for reconciliation with the world."[111] Grace, then, is not God's "Yes" to our "no," but neither is it God's "Yes" without the "No." The fact that every human has been justified by grace exposes our dire need and inability to provide grace for ourselves; the more the grace is poured out, the more the need is exposed. Grace is "utterly free," notes T. F. Torrance, "but it is so difficult because its absolute freeness devalues the moral and religious currency which we have minted at such cost out of our own self-understanding. It is too costly for us."[112]

Torrance further helps us to understand how grace can be both free and costly:

> Because God has concluded us all under His mercy and justified us freely through grace, all men are put on the same level, for whether they are good or bad, religious or secular, within the Church or the world, they all alike come under the total judgement of grace, the judgement that everything they are and have is wholly called into question simply by the fact that they are saved by grace alone. This grace is infinitely costly to God because it is grace through the blood of Christ, but it is desperately costly to man because it lays the axe to the root of all his cherished possessions and achievements, not least in the realm of his religion, for it is in religion that man's self-justification may reach its supreme and most subtle form.[113]

To say that Christ took our place without acknowledging what "our place" is is to hear the "Yes" without the "No." It is to be ignorant or apathetic toward one's personal complicity in the costliness of grace and to deny one's utter unworthiness in light of utterly free grace. Whatever attitude this may be, and it can take many forms, it is not belief for Bonhoeffer and Barth. Belief cannot come until we recognize, in Bonhoeffer's words, that "it is *we* who are crucified with him." Barth proclaims in this same vein:

---

111. Bonhoeffer, *Ethics*, 56.

112. T. F. Torrance, "Cheap and Costly Grace," 300–301.

113. Ibid., 290. Elsewhere Torrance calls grace "the crisis of religion" (T. F. Torrance, *Karl Barth: Introduction*, 70).

> Look at Jesus on the cross, accused, sentenced and punished in-
> stead of us! Do you know for whose sake he is hanging there? For
> *our* sake—because of *our* sin—sharing *our* captivity—burdened
> with *our* suffering! He nails *our* life to the cross. This is how God
> had to deal with *us*. From this darkness he has saved *us*. He who
> is not shattered after hearing this news may not yet have grasped
> the word of God: *By grace you have been saved.*[114]

"No one can be proud of being saved," continues Barth. "Each one can
only fold his hands in great lowliness of heart and be thankful like a
child."[115] This is the attitude of one who, by the Spirit, has ears to hear the
"No" in the "Yes," one who understands the cost intrinsic to the grace.
This is what Bonhoeffer meant by his statement, "When Christ calls a
man to himself, he bids him to come and die."

Any Christianity that causes us to lighten the gravity of our sin is
Christianity without Christ; it is deceptive and harmful, states Barth.
The "dear" grace of Jesus Christ "does not lessen our accusation and
sentence" but overwhelms it. The doctrine of the atonement can be dan-
gerously misunderstood if "there is no knowledge and proclamation of
what has actually been done by God under this name. . . . The fact that
it speaks of God making good what we have spoiled does not mean that
we can call evil good."[116] It is this kind of phony faith, the "Yes" to the
"no" or the "Yes" without the "No," that Bonhoeffer rails against in *The
Cost of Discipleship.*

If there remains any confusion over what Bonhoeffer was aiming
for in this book, his words from the end of chapter 1 should be sufficient
to dispel it:

> Happy are they who have reached the end of the road we seek
> to tread, who are astonished to discover the by no means self-
> evident truth that grace is costly just because it is the grace of
> God in Jesus Christ. Happy are the simple followers of Jesus
> Christ who have been overcome by his grace, and are able to sing
> the praises of the all-sufficient grace of Christ with humbleness
> of heart. Happy are they who, knowing that grace, can live in
> the world without being of it, who, by following Jesus Christ, are
> so assured of their heavenly citizenship that they are truly free
> to live their lives in this world. Happy are they who know that

114. Barth, "By Grace," 38. Sermon delivered August 14, 1955.
115. Ibid., 39.
116. Barth, *CD* 4/1:69–70.

discipleship simply means the life which springs from grace, and that grace simply means discipleship.[117]

CONCLUSION: TRUE RESPONSE-ABILITY IN CHRIST

What can we now say, then, about grace, belief, and obedience? God's grace in Jesus Christ is free. The problem, as Bonhoeffer and Barth saw it, is not that grace is complete and free, but that it is not believed. Belief in Jesus Christ means a belief that he has exhaustively accomplished our salvation in his own person. Faith comes by hearing the "Yes" and the "No" together; by the Spirit we recognize that we are *justified sinners,* "loved, condemned and reconciled in Christ."[118] Gratefully secure in Christ's unconditional acceptance, we are liberated to a new life of joyful participation in and dependence on our Savior. As Ray Anderson says, it is in this way that unconditional grace leads to unconditional obedience; belief and obedience are "two sides of the same coin."[119] Now we understand Bonhoeffer's words, "only he who believes is obedient, and only he who is obedient believes."

We have seen that justification by grace is about Jesus Christ from beginning to end. This is so because of the ontological significance of the incarnation. But what we are only now beginning to see is something even greater, something driven by the inseparability of belief and obedience. We are discovering that the ontological depths of the incarnation

117. Bonhoeffer, *Cost of Discipleship,* 47.

118. Bonhoeffer, *Ethics,* 192. "Loved, condemned and reconciled" is a favorite phrase of Bonhoeffer's; see also 202. Barth asserts that it is at the point of personal identification with the Rejected One that the Holy Spirit works: "But it is only when there is no hope—and the Rejected on Golgotha, and the rejected in ourselves . . . has no hope—that there is real hope, for it is only there that the work of the Holy Spirit can intervene and proclamation can become really comprehensible and faith really alive" (Barth, *CD* 2/2:458). The gospel of grace is a judgment of grace, and therefore its proclamation has a performative element, i.e., "it aims at transformation" (Jones, *Embodying Forgiveness,* 136).

119. Anderson, personal correspondence. Of "only he who is obedient believes," Geoffrey B. Kelly adds: "Bonhoeffer was not arguing that liberating faith needs to be supplemented by some action. Rather, he saw the whole sphere of Christian obedience to God's will in any age inextricably bound to faith and the gospel of what God has done for us in Christ. Faith and obedience are linked together in a dialectical and indissoluble unity, in which willingness to obey and serve God is the natural and spontaneous note of a life governed by dedication to the person and mission of Jesus Christ" (Kelly, *Liberating Faith,* 62).

cannot be limited to justification; that as the only reality, Jesus Christ fills the sphere of all of our existence. As Elected Man, Jesus Christ is sanctified man;[120] he has accomplished not only our justification but our sanctification. To walk in the reality of our sanctification is to walk freely by faith in the Spirit, spontaneously fulfilling the law.

Like incarnation and atonement, and revelation and reconciliation, justification and sanctification cannot be separated.[121] Jesus does it all. "What are we to do?" asks Barth:

> We are to accept it as right that God is our righteousness.... What was done with us in Jesus Christ was that God made Himself our righteousness: in defiance of our defiance, in opposition to our opposition. Our required conformity with the action of divine grace is that we accept it as right, as the upper part of the Yes and No in which we move; that our action be played out under and within the frame of this divine action. This is the content of the divine claim on all men.[122]

Once we have come alive to our justification in hearing the divine "Yes" and "No" together, understanding that we are undeservedly elected because of Christ's "Yes" to the Father on our behalf, we may now participate with our own "yes" in the "Yes" of our brother. At the same time, we can be sure that in God's faithful sanctifying love God will chasten us, continuing to say "No" to our "no" until we find the freedom of the participatory "yes."

Bonhoeffer stresses that we need to acknowledge *who* does the work *without* our participation before we can freely participate ourselves: "I am met in his work as one who cannot possibly do the work he does. It is through his work that I recognize the gracious God."[123] Our life in Christ is truly *in Christ*; it is ontologically structured. From within this

---

120. Barth, *CD* 2/2:740.

121. Ibid., 4/2:505. For Barth, Christ did not come only to die for us but to live for us. To ignore the indissoluble relationship between justification and sanctification is to deny the view of the full-orbed ontological significance of the incarnation, which he shares with Bonhoeffer. This leads to corresponding errors: "to the idea of God who works in isolation, and His 'cheap grace'(D. Bonhoeffer), and therefore an indolent quietism, where the relationship of justification to sanctification is neglected; and to that of a favoured man who works in isolation, and therefore to an illusory activism, where the relationship of sanctification to justification is forgotten."

122. Ibid., 2/2:582.

123. Cited in Jones, *Embodying Forgiveness*, 156.

structure, under this "easy" yoke, we allow ourselves "to be caught up in the way of Jesus, into the messianic event."[124] In *Ethics* we read: "The question of good becomes the question of participation in the divine reality which is revealed in Christ."[125] "The actions of the Christian . . . spring from joy in the accomplishment of the reconciliation of the world with God; they spring from the peace which comes with the completion of the work of salvation in Jesus Christ; they spring from the all-embracing life which is Jesus Christ."[126] Discipleship, then, is response-ability, a response to grace!

Barth reminds us that as response-able disciples we enjoy "an ultimate and profound irresponsibility" under the light yoke of Jesus;[127] to love God "means to become what we already are, those who are loved by Him";[128] obedience becomes "a happy obligation";[129] the command of God "a festive occasion,"[130] "a permission"[131]—no longer "you shall but you may."[132] Finally, "What is a liberation for new action which does not rest from the very outset and continually on the forgiveness of sins? Who can and will serve God but the child of God who lives by the promise of his unmerited adoption?"[133]

Karl Barth and Dietrich Bonhoeffer basked in their identity as sons of God by grace, and they encouraged others to likewise recognize the reality of their filial belonging in Christ. We now close our study with

---

124. Bonhoeffer, *Letters and Papers*, 361. Bonhoeffer says here: "It is not the religious act that makes the Christian, but participation in the sufferings of God in the secular life."

125. Bonhoeffer, *Ethics*, 163.

126. Ibid., 191. Bonhoeffer and Barth were both keen to implement the metaphor of the yoke. For a classic passage in Barth regarding the light burden of participation, see *CD* 1/2:274–75: "Our participation does not depend upon our fitness for this work. It is a participation in spite of our unsuitability. It rests upon the forgiveness of sins. It is grace. . . . That is just why it is not a participation which involves anxiety and worry whether we can really do what we are required to do. Of course we cannot do it. That is the presupposition of our participation."

127. Barth, *CD* 1/2:274.

128. Ibid., 389.

129. Ibid., 385.

130. Ibid., 2/2:588.

131. Ibid., 585.

132. Barth, "You May," 23. Sermon delivered April 3, 1960.

133. Barth, *CD* 4/2:505.

choice words of these two friends—the teacher, speaking to prisoners; the student, a prisoner.

> Do you know who you really are? . . . Because the old man—you know him well enough—has already been extinguished in the death of Jesus, because you may no longer be this old man, because your own case has been disposed of by the power of Jesus' death, therefore you yourself are now the new man, loved by God, chosen, saved and accepted by him who has said to you and will say to you his divine "yes." Take courage; this is what you are.[134]

Who am I? They mock me,
  these lonely questions of mine.
Whoever I am,
  thou knowest, O God, I am thine.[135]

134. Barth, "Teach Us," 123.

135. Bonhoeffer, *Letters and Papers*, 348.

Chapter 3
Introduction

"Go with the Spirit!"

I N THIS CHAPTER I would like to elaborate on the subject of prayer from within its vibrant trinitarian context as a key illustration of everything I have been saying up to this point. Because of our anthropocentric tendencies, prayer has often been thought of as something we human beings say to a God "out there." The notion of prayer to God being sourced *in* God has unfortunately been underemphasized. Together I hope we might entertain anew the exciting ramifications of the idea that, in the vein of Paul and the vernacular of Torrance, it is no longer I who pray, but Christ who prays in me.

At St. Andrews I attended the first official course on the Holy Spirit to be offered since the inception of the divinity school in 1539. Fortunate for me was the fact that the senior teacher for the course was Professor Jeremy Begbie, who, having himself been mentored by J. B. Torrance, was intimately acquainted with my theological project. Jeremy helped me to understand how a robust theology of the Spirit protects us against a static ontology, for while the Holy Spirit opens us up and particularizes the gospel to us, he never does so in violation of his economy of love or in a way that manipulates or depersonalizes us.[1] Jeremy taught with charisma and musical passion, and his personal charge to "Go with the Spirit" still rings in my ears.

Admittedly, as with past course catalogues at St. Andrews, the first two chapters of this volume have not given an abundance of attention to the Holy Spirit. In a way, that seems appropriate, because the Spirit is

---

1. On the contrary, linear or logico-causal notions such as "irresistible grace" and universalism are built on static inevitabilities and therefore impinge on the freedom of the Spirit and on the God-given integrity of free human response.

always trying to direct our gaze most particularly toward God incarnate. This chapter, however, offers a careful look at the theology of the Holy Spirit, especially as it relates to prayer. To me, this is a most natural connection, because of the synonymous nature of the biblical words *Spirit*, *wind*, and *breath*.

One of the most transforming elements in my own prayer life has been the acknowledgment that I am involuntarily implicated in prayer that is, very much like my breathing, incessant. In recent years I have relished quiet moments to focus intentionally on the ins and outs of my breathing, relating them to what I know to be the trinitarian dynamic at play because of my union with Christ by grace. As I breathe in I imagine the words from the Father to me, "I love you son," or "I love you Jeff," and then, as I breathe out, "I love you Father," the words of Christ's response *for* me. In this exercise I am heightened in my awareness that grace is always going on, and hearing the Spirit's whispers of grace has the effect of centering me in the knowledge that my life is lived not only to God but also from God. As we have seen, to be carried along by grace in this way is to know the peace that promotes participation in the direction of true human freedom, from the Son to the Father by the Spirit.

In the course of what follows, familiar themes from the previous chapters will reappear—retrospective and prospective salvation (being saved from and saved for), the wonderful exchange, the assumption of fallen humanity by the doctor who became the patient while remaining the doctor, and others. I hope the familiarity of these themes, far from breeding contempt, will be like the recognition of old friends who can only help to advance us toward a clearer understanding of trinitarian prayer.

In assessing the context and role for praying believers, we will look closely at Paul's letter to the Christians in Rome. As in our exegesis of any of the Epistles, however, we should not let our talk about believers preclude the ontological truth of the double movement for all persons, believers and unbelievers alike. If we have learned anything in our study, it is the premise that the strong currents of grace are always flowing. Christian belief should not be perceived as adding to the truth, as if we (or even the Holy Spirit) were finishing a work Christ had not finished.

This chapter keeps with the description of a Christian as one who desires to participate in the human-Godward current of truth and correctly attributes it to Christ. In this view, prayer, like all other Christian activity, is something we are caught up in, not something we create. Maybe Paul's encouragement to "pray without ceasing" is his way of urging our participation in the incessant prayers of Spirit and Son on our behalf. Regardless, prayer in Christ is perhaps our profoundest way of "going with the Ghost," worshiping the Father together in spirit and in truth.

Chapter 3

Prayer as Grace

Jesus suffers in His Passion the pains which men inflict upon Him; but in His Agony He suffers those that He inflicts upon Himself. . . .

Jesus has no one on earth to feel and share His pain or even to know of it; only Heaven and He share that knowledge. Jesus in a garden; not of delights like the first Adam, where he lost himself and the human race, but in a garden of agony, where He saves Himself and the whole race. He suffers this anguish and this desertion in the horror of night.

. . . Then He complained as though He could not contain His weight of grief: "My soul is sorrowful to death." . . .

. . . He prays only once that the cup should pass, and even then with submission; and twice, that it should come if it ought.

Jesus in weariness.

Jesus, seeing all His friends sleeping, all his enemies awake, commits Himself utterly to the Father. . . .

Jesus in agony and the sharpest pains, prays longer.

—Blaise Pascal, *Mystery of Jesus*[1]

PASCAL'S VIVID PORTRAIT OF Jesus in the garden reminds us that we have a God who has identified with us on the deepest level. Here we find him Word and flesh, Judge and judged, Son of God and Son of Man, groaning in the Spirit, "Abba, Father" (Mark 14:36). How strange—God as the subject and object of prayer; how defiant to our cognitive senses. The dubious Arius declared, "He cannot be both God and a man praying to God!" To which Athanasius retorted, "Arius, you do not understand the meaning of grace."[2]

---

1. Quoted by Mortimer, *Pascal*, 225–27.
2. J. B. Torrance, *Worship, Community*, 54.

It will be the aim of this chapter to set forth the idea of prayer as grace. Fundamentally, all Christian prayer is within the circle of Christ's own self-offering to the Father on our behalf. Now by the Spirit of sonship believers may participate in Christ's prayers to the Father, for Christ *really* inhabits the prayers of the saints. We are caught up into the double movement of grace from the Father, through the Son and in the Spirit, and back again through the Son to the Father. It is this wonderful promise, that our prayers to God are actually the prayers of God, that Paul expounds mightily in Romans chapter 8.

Romans 8 is the most "inspired" chapter in the epistle. "Spirit" occurs twenty-one times in this section, while only thirteen times in all the rest of the book.[3] "The work of the Spirit in Romans 8," notes James Dunn, "is Paul's climactic account of the way the grace of God comes to clearest and fullest effect in believers." Paul spends the first third of the chapter outlining the roles of "the Spirit of life" as liberator against the powers of sin and death (8:2) and enabler of godly conduct in believers (8:4–6, 13). The indwelling Spirit is the true life-giver (8:10–11).[4]

C. K. Barrett has said, "The fundamental context of thought in which Paul places the Holy Spirit is eschatology,"[5] and verses 14 and 15 of chapter 8 transition into what Gordon Fee has called "one of Paul's finest hours" regarding his eschatological thinking.[6] The Apostle stretches his canvas over the poles of the two apparently contradictory "adoptions"— "For you did not receive a spirit that makes you a slave again to fear, but you received the Spirit of sonship" (8:15); and "we ourselves, who have the firstfruits of the Spirit, groan inwardly as we wait eagerly for our adoption as sons" (8:23). Thus Paul defines his hearers' existence as within an "already but not yet" tension.[7] Returning to C. K. Barrett:

> Thus the Spirit bears witness that we are children of God; but this is not an end in itself; it points on to a further truth. If you are your father's child you are your father's heir, and may at some time expect to receive more than you already have by way of patrimony. We are thus joint-heirs with our elder Brother. This means

---

3. Cranfield, *Romans*, 172. The word appears five times in chapters 1–7, and eight times in chapters 9–16.

4. Dunn, "Spirit Speech," 82.

5. Barrett, *Paul*, 131.

6. Fee, *God's Empowering Presence*, 571.

7. Moo, *Romans*, 501.

the future; clearly we have not yet entered upon the inheritance.
... [Firstfruits] means the installment of a payment—both a part
of the total price, and the pledge that the rest will be paid in due
course. This is perhaps the clearest of all the terms Paul uses to
denote the place of the Spirit in his eschatological system.[8]

It is from within this overlap of the ages that believers suffer and
groan with the rest of creation for the final redemption and the complete
manifestation of the new order, "liberated from its bondage to decay"
(8:21). It is also from within this tension that we have *hope*, a word full
of content for the early church; "it did not mean mere wishfulness but
absolute certainty," reminds Fee.[9] It is in the Spirit that we have the hope
of glory and "God's empowering presence in the context of our present
weaknesses."[10] Douglas Moo helpfully describes the Spirit's central role
in meeting us in our inchoate existence: "'Already,' through the indwelling presence of God's Spirit, we have been transferred into the new age
of blessing and salvation; but the very fact that the Spirit is only the 'first
fruits' makes us sadly conscious that we have 'not yet' severed all ties to
the old age of sin and death."[11]

Interestingly, as Moo alludes, it is precisely because the Spirit in-
dwells us that we are so aware of the not-fully-worked-out status of our
lives. While we "wait eagerly," we "groan inwardly" (8:23). Far from being
reactive, the Spirit acts upon us, taking the initiative in God's economy of
salvation to strengthen our "sense of dis-ease" and to amplify our yearn-
ings for final healing. "The image of groaning," notes Dunn, " implies
thought of discomfort, irritation, frustration, even pain."[12]

Thankfully, as children of promise we can trust with Paul that "our
present sufferings are not worth comparing with the glory that will be
revealed in us" (8:18). Yet we are not meant to be in this world simply
biding our time, apathetically twiddling our thumbs until the culmination of the kingdom. If, as Colin Gunton has emphasized, the Spirit's
distinctive function is to perfect the creation, "to bring to completion
that for which each person and thing is created,"[13] then we as believ-

8. Barrett, *Paul*, 132.

9. Fee, *Paul*, 61.

10. Fee, *God's Empowering Presence*, 579.

11. Moo, *Romans*, 520.

12. Dunn, "Spirit Speech," 87.

13. Gunton, *One*, 189.

ers may participate in what is already an ongoing renewal process. "The notion that this life is no more than a preparation for a life beyond," notes Jurgen Moltmann, "is the theory of a refusal to live, and a religious fraud. It is inconsistent with the living God, who is 'a lover of life.'"[14] In their book *Hope against Hope: Christian Eschatology in Contemporary Context*, Trevor Hart and Richard Bauckham discuss this matter of "the future-made-present":

> In our daily struggle with the patterns and forces of death, the Holy Spirit of life both sets us free from the bonds of the past and empowers us to move forward in hope, breathing new life into our shrivelled capacities and opening them up to receive a flow of power from God's promised future . . . , taking seriously the possibility of the advent of new and unpredictable manifestations of what will finally be, in the midst of the here-and-now. We live, in other words, in a present which is shaped by the future rather than the past, in the power of what we might call the future-made-present.[15]

Christopher Cocksworth has made a similar observation: "The eschatological work of the Spirit also involves bringing God's future to bear on our present, not only by identifying the gap between what is and what is to come, but also by breaking God's future into our present in order to close the gap."[16] How do believers best participate in this gap-closing? Interestingly, for Hart, Bauckham, and Cocksworth, "eschatological activism" begins with prayer.[17] *Thy Kingdom come, Thy will be done, on earth as it is in heaven. . . .*

PAUL'S MOST INSPIRED CHAPTER

It is certainly no coincidence that it is within Romans 8, a section where "Spirit" is the key word, that Paul chooses to present his theology of prayer.

> In the same way, the Spirit helps us in our weakness. We do not know what we ought to pray for, but the Spirit himself intercedes for us with groans that words cannot express. And he who searches our hearts knows the mind of the Spirit, because the Spirit intercedes for the saints in accordance with God's will. (8:26–27)

14. Cited in Hart and Bauckham, *Hope against Hope*, 198.

15. Hart and Bauckham, *Hope against Hope*, 198.

16. Cocksworth, *Holy, Holy, Holy*, 196.

17. Hart and Bauckham, *Hope against Hope*, 202.

Commentators have spent many pages unpacking these two verses. Joseph Fitzmyer has detected the idea of the Spirit as intercessor to be a "Pauline novelty" not found elsewhere in all of Scripture or in any pre-Christian Jewish literature. In this passage, asserts Fitzmyer, Paul "recognizes the Spirit's ineffable sighs as the source of all genuine Christian prayer. Such assistance is not limited to the prayer of petition, but would include all manner of communing with God, be it doxology in adoration, blessing, praise, thanksgiving, penitent confession, supplication, or above all, acknowledgment of God as Father."[18]

Earlier we considered the Spirit's role in sharpening and even exacerbating our painful awareness of the "already–not yet" in our lives and environment. Here we see the Comforter coming alongside us in our predicament, undergirding us with his own groans of intercession. The Spirit's helpfulness highlights our helplessness. Indeed, we do not even know what prayers to pray, much less how to pray them! As James D. G. Dunn has said, "Here the believer is in an even worse state than the 'I' of 7:14–24. The 'I' knew what to do, . . . but failed. Here the problem is different: . . . [believers] do not know what to want."[19] Theologian Tom Smail adds: "It is encouraging to us lesser mortals to see that even Paul starts from recognition of much weakness and incapacity precisely in relation to prayer, the central point of our relationship to God." A belief in Spirit-strengthened prayer should encourage participation, not passivity, in the believer, for "the divine activity in us is the presupposition of the human activity, rather than the other way around. It is not that we pray so that the Spirit can work in us; it is because the Spirit is already at work within us that we can pray."[20]

The fact that Paul regularly urges believers to pray without this caveat (about not knowing what to pray) has led some interpreters to see Paul's emphasis in verse 26 to be more about the manner than the content of prayer; it refers to our inadequacy concerning *how* to pray rightly. Believers struggle to discern what God's will might be in any given situation, desiring to align their petitions with God's mind on the matter. This interpretation is predicated on the following verse, which speaks of the Spirit interceding for us "in accordance with God's will." It is for this very reason, claims Douglas Moo, that all of our requests to God

18. Fitzmyer, *Romans*, 518.

19. Dunn, "Spirit Speech," 89.

20. Smail, *Giving Gift*, 204.

must be qualified by "if it is in accordance with your will." Regardless of one's view as to Paul's meaning, the bottom line is that all of our prayers are conditioned by our inability and enabled by the Spirit's ability.[21] Our prayers might not be God's will, but thankfully the Spirit's always are.

> When we do not know what to pray for—yes, even when we pray things that are not best for us—we need not despair, for we can depend on the Spirit's ministry of perfect intercession "on our behalf." Here is one potent source for that "patient fortitude" with which we are to await our glory (v. 25); . . . our failure to understand God's purposes and plans, to see "the beginning from the end," does not mean that effective, powerful prayer for our specific needs is absent.[22]

We will return to this subject of God's will in prayer at a later point. But another divisive issue concerning prayer in 8:26–27 revolves around the nature of the Spirit's groans: Are they *really* the Spirit's? Or is this simply another way of saying that believers groan, albeit with the Spirit's help? Paul has already mentioned the believers' groans three verses earlier: "We who have the firstfruits of the Spirit groan inwardly." To further complicate matters, some view Paul as referring to glossolalia in 8:26–27, as he does elsewhere when speaking of prayer in the Spirit. The bulk of the scholarship suggests that within the context of Romans, the groanings are best understood, not as believers' own and not as glossolalia, but as the Spirit's: "It is preferable to understand these groans as the Spirit's own 'language of prayer,' a ministry of intercession that takes place in our hearts in a manner imperceptible to us."[23]

In a manner worth repeating, James Dunn has this to say about the beautiful Spirit-dynamic of Romans 8:26–27:

> It is the Spirit speaking with primal speech, putting believers in touch with their deepest being where language fails, expressing the instinctive recognition of the creature that its existence depends solely and ultimately on God alone. It is the Spirit stripping the human creature of all the pride and pretense which human

21. Moo, *Romans*, 524.

22. Ibid., 526.

23. Ibid., 525–26. Contra Moo and others, Gordon Fee asserts: "Origen probably had it right in understanding these sentences . . . to refer to a kind of private ('to oneself') praying in tongues that Paul speaks about as part of his resolution of the practice of uninterpreted tongues in the worshipping community in Corinth" (Fee, *God's Empowering Presence*, 580; see the discussion on 577–86).

ability with words brings, of all the power to persuade and charm, to manipulate and deceive which human speech makes possible. This is the cry of the creature both acknowledging its creatureliness and confessing God as its God.

. . . It functions as effective prayer. Why? Because God is at both ends of the process. The Spirit is in tune with God. That is, the Spirit working deep at the root of human inarticulateness, the Spirit working deep at the root of creation's futility and the believer's frustration, is working with God, as part of and in accordance with God's will (8:27). Because the heart is where the inner reality of the person is, the openness and opening of the heart to God is an effective communication with God and succeeds in keeping open the channels of grace between believers and God. At this point Spirit speech and heart language are one.[24]

Thus far we have explored the middle portion of Romans 8 in some detail, but we have barely begun to get a full-orbed grasp of Paul's theology of prayer in the chapter. Our focus has been on the eschatological and gap-closing significance of the Holy Spirit in 8:14–27, with special emphasis on the Spirit's intercession in and for us. There is one, however, who has been conspicuously absent from our discussion—the Lord Jesus Christ—and it is only when we couch 8:14–27 in its scriptural environs that the crucial trinitarian import of the passage becomes plain, for all prayer in the Spirit to the Father must be through the Son.

Tom Smail offers a valuable insight on Romans 8:26–27 in his book *The Giving Gift*. "We are invited to see prayer," he says, "not primarily as a duty required of us, but much more as a gift given to us by the Holy Spirit: God on our side of the relationship. Paul does not speak of what we ourselves are to do about praying, but rather of what God is doing about it on our behalf."[25] This statement traces the path we have trodden thus far, but taken in and of itself, it is an anemic description of Paul's theology of prayer in Romans 8. As we shall see, what God is *doing* on our behalf has everything to do with what God has *done* in the person of Jesus Christ.

As a matter of fact, we might say that while "Spirit" is the key word in Romans 8, Jesus Christ is the main character. Lest I draw the ire of trinitarian scholars bent on desynonymizing, or making room for the

24. Dunn, "Spirit Speech," 90, 89–90.

25. Smail, *Giving Gift*, 205. As we shall see, Smail goes on to develop a fully trinitarian view of prayer.

differentiated *hypostasis* of the Spirit, I must hasten to add that I am not promoting the Spirit as the alter ego of Christ, but rather the idea that the Holy Spirit is virtually inseparable from the ongoing vicarious humanity of Christ in the experience of believers. In proceeding to apprehend Paul's theology of prayer, we must acknowledge the elements of trinitarian unity and diversity within Romans 8.

> You, however, are controlled not by the sinful nature but by the Spirit, if the Spirit of God lives in you. And if anyone does not have the Spirit of Christ, he does not belong to Christ. But if Christ is in you, your body is dead because of sin, yet your spirit is alive because of righteousness. And if the Spirit of him who raised Jesus from the dead is living in you, he who raised Christ from the dead will also give life to your mortal bodies through his Spirit, who lives in you. (8:9–11)

From the passage above, it appears that we could construct the formulation *Spirit of God = Spirit of Christ = Christ in you.*[26] Indeed, the apparent ease with which Paul moves from one term to another has caused critics to take pause. Especially troublesome is what appears to be a conflation of the Spirit and Christ. C. K. Barrett sets the stage for our investigation into the trinitarian dynamics reflected in the chapter: "That Paul clearly defined and differentiated the second and third persons of the Trinity cannot possibly be maintained; neither however did he simply identify them. Both their proximity to each other and their distinction are shown in Romans 8:8–11."[27]

While it is true that Paul comes closest of all New Testament writers to equating the Holy Spirit and Christ,[28] surely we cannot say that he is guilty of synonymizing. The phrase "Spirit of Christ" itself connotes some kind of difference (versus simply "Christ"), but how much? Is it negligible? Is the Spirit, as some have asserted, simply the mode of existence of the risen Christ in the world? Whether justified or not, even eminent theologians like Karl Barth have been called to task for remarks such as the following: "The Holy Spirit is the Spirit of Jesus Christ. . . . The Holy Spirit is nothing

---

26. Dodd, *Romans*, 123.

27. Barrett, *Paul*, 133.

28. Other examples include Gal 4:6, "Spirit of his Son"; Phil 1:19, "Spirit of Jesus Christ"; 2 Cor 3:17, "the Lord is the Spirit . . . Spirit of the Lord"; also 1 Cor 15:45, "the last Adam, a life-giving spirit."

else than a certain relation of the Word to man."[29] Obviously, if the work of the Spirit is merely a description of Christ's ongoing ministry in a *spiritual way*, then trinitarianism collapses into binitarianism.[30]

Others have warned against a sense of subordinationism in the phrase "Spirit of Christ," as if it speaks of a Spirit dominated by Christ's authority. This is a reaction against those who want to uphold Christ as the "Lord of the Spirit" and a "controlling factor in pneumatology."[31] Interestingly, it is in the Gospel record that we see anything but a subordinate role of the Spirit. According to Gary Badcock, the Spirit's work should always be characterized by Christ, but in a more positive and reciprocal way: "The Spirit . . . is not only the Spirit given by Christ, or the Spirit under his control, but it is also the Spirit who rested on Jesus in such a way as to make him what he was. . . . We can speak of the 'Christlike' Spirit, but only because the Spirit has *already* defined the character of Jesus. . . . In short, Christ is as much like the Spirit as the Spirit is like Christ."[32] Jurgen Moltmann is another scholar who is concerned about the Holy Spirit being stamped as a second-class citizen in the Trinity. He asserts that the procession of the Spirit from the Father was at least simultaneous with if not primary to the begetting of the Son; and therefore: "Christ's experience of the Spirit as it is narrated, and the proclaimed experience of Christ in the Spirit, do not simply follow one another in time. They are interlocked through the structure of the Trinity."[33]

This concept of transition regarding Christ's experience of the Spirit and the experience of Christ in the Spirit can help us out of the muddle and get us back to Paul's meaning in Romans 8. I have posited that in the strictest sense Paul is not subsuming the Spirit into Christ by his use of "the Spirit of Christ"; neither would I suggest that he relegates the Spirit to inferior status. With the resurrection, ascension, and Pentecost, there was a pneumatic "turning of the corner," whereby the Spirit who inspired Jesus became defined and understood as the Spirit of Christ.

---

29. Barth, *Dogmatics in Outline*, 138.

30. See Smail, *Giving Gift*, 41, where he critiques Hendrickus Berkhof's statement that "the Spirit is the new way of existence and action by Jesus Christ . . . , continuing and making effective on a world-wide scale what he began in his earthly life."

31. Dunn, *Christology*, 17.

32. Badcock, *Light of Truth*, 160.

33. Moltmann, *Spirit of Life*, 60. Moltmann's view would obviously not be shared by those who prefer the later, *filioque*, version of the Nicene Creed, where the Spirit is said to proceed "from the Father *and the Son*."

Therefore, Paul could make a virtual identification between Christ and the Spirit based on the *believer's experience*, because "one cannot experience Christ without experiencing Spirit. Or to put it more accurately: one cannot experience Christ except as Spirit, which also means that one cannot experience Spirit except as Christ."[34] Again, it must be stressed that in Paul's doctrine this was not a functional identification (i.e., synonymizing of persons) but more an existential one.

Indeed, this view brings us full circle, because now we can read Paul's "unstudied movement" from "Spirit of God" to "Spirit of Christ" to "Christ" to "Spirit" in Romans 8:9–11 with full confidence in the Apostle's "practical trinitarianism." At the same time, though, holding fast to a differentiation of persons in this passage does introduce us to one other issue that needs to be addressed, because it seems to dictate the interesting if awkward concept that the Spirit and Christ both indwell us ("if Christ is in you," 8:10; "if the Spirit of him who raised Jesus from the dead is living in you," 8:11). Douglas Moo contributes these insights:

> What this means is not that Christ and the Spirit are equated or interchangeable, but that Christ and the Spirit are so closely related in communicating to believers the benefits of salvation that Paul can move from one to the other almost unconsciously. Again, it is clear that the believer . . . has not only Christ but also the Spirit resident within. . . . The indwelling Spirit and the indwelling Christ are distinguishable but inseparable.[35]

Are we prepared to adopt such a stance—both Christ and the Spirit indwelling us? What about the unity and oneness of persons? Is this too much differentiation? At this stage one is reminded that trinitarian theology is very much like trying to close an overstuffed suitcase. Just when you manage to solve one side, clothes leak out the other! Perhaps

---

34. Dunn, *Jesus and the Spirit*, 323. This solution is helpful as long as we resist collapsing the Spirit and Christ back into each other. Gary Badcock cautions: "Both the fact that Christ does not fill the whole sphere of deity in Paul's thought and the fact that a plurality of some sort in Paul's God, and certainly in Paul's religious experience, must be admitted. The Spirit within and the risen Christ beyond are not one but two. . . . We may say that for Paul, the Spirit is as much the Spirit of the Father as he is the Spirit of the Son" (Badcock, *Light of Truth*, 26). I would countercaution Badcock against simplistic differentiation and ask, "What about *Christ* within?"

35. Moo, *Romans*, 491. The issue of Christ and the Spirit being present in unbelievers entails an ontological interpretation that is not in view here and that, if addressed, would not be encouraged by Moo.

Gordon Fee's interpretation on this same passage can help us to find a middle way between differentiation and modalism:

> Everything about the argument and the context suggests that "Christ in you" is simply Pauline shorthand for "the Spirit of Christ in you," or perhaps better in this case, "Christ in you by his Spirit." That is, it is doubtful either that Paul has made some kind of "identification" of the risen Christ with the Spirit so that his language reflects that confusion, or that Paul somehow envisioned both Christ and the Spirit indwelling the believer, "side by side" as it were. Rather, very much as in Ephesians 2:22, where the church is seen as the "habitation of God" by the Spirit, so here the believer is the "habitation" of Christ, also by the Spirit.[36]

In light of both comments, we may be drawn to Moo's idea of Spirit and Christ being "distinguishable but inseparable," while holding to Fee's tenet of Christ dwelling in the believer *by* the Spirit. Regardless, it is this closest of associations between Jesus Christ and the Spirit that will be critical for us as we move forward in the quest to grasp Paul's doctrine of prayer as grace in Romans 8.

BUILDING ON A CHRISTOLOGICAL ASSUMPTION

I have been pointing toward the idea that prayer in the Spirit cannot be understood without its christological basis, and now we must lay some necessary groundwork. Fundamental to any understanding of prayer as grace is the overarching concept of grace that comes to us in the person of Jesus Christ. It is the doctrine of the vicarious humanity of Christ that takes most seriously the incarnational truth that God came as man, took on our diseased, fallen flesh—humanity at its very worst—and sanctified it from within by his perfectly obedient life and death and victorious resurrection in the power of the Holy Spirit. His humanity is vicarious because Christ did it all as our representative and for our sake, that we might live in Christ and participate by faith in what he has already accomplished for us once for all. This is the truth Paul communicates in the opening verses of Romans 8:

> Therefore, there is now no condemnation for those who are in Christ Jesus, because through Christ Jesus the law of the Spirit of life set me free from the law of sin and death. *For what the law was powerless to do in that it was weakened by the sinful nature,*

36. Fee, *God's Empowering Presence*, 548.

*God did by sending his own Son in the likeness of sinful man to be
a sin offering. And so he condemned sin in sinful man,* in order
that the righteous requirements of the law might be fully met in
us, who do not live according to the sinful nature but according
to the Spirit. (8:1–4)

Because of all that hinges upon it, Romans 8:3 (in italics) is argu-
ably the most critical verse in the chapter. "This is the closest expression in Pauline writings to the idea of incarnation, which is otherwise
a Johannine way of expressing the coming of Christ," asserts Joseph
Fitzmyer.[37] What exactly does it mean that the Father sent his Son "in
the likeness of sinful man," or, as it is more often translated, "in the likeness of sinful flesh?"

To begin with, we must hold on to the truth that Jesus Christ was
the God-man; our portrait of him must include his full divinity as well as
his true humanity. While taking on our fallen human nature, he always
remained Himself (capitalized for emphasis). The early church went to
great pains to protect the integrity of the incarnation, insisting that Jesus
Christ was one person, two natures. From the Chalcedonian Definition
of Faith (451) we read:

> Wherefore, following the holy Fathers, we all with one voice con-
> fess our Lord Jesus Christ one and the same Son, the same perfect
> in Godhead, the same perfect in manhood, truly God and truly
> man, the same consisting of a reasonable soul and a body, of one
> substance with the Father as touching the Godhead, the same
> of one substance with us as touching the manhood, *like us in all
> things apart from sin*; begotten of the Father before the ages as
> touching the Godhead, the same in the last days, for us and for our
> salvation, born from the Virgin Mary, the *Theotokos,* as touching
> the manhood, one and the same Christ, Son, Lord, Only-begotten,
> to be acknowledged in two natures, without confusion, without
> change, without division, without separation; the distinction of
> natures being in no way abolished because of the union, but rather
> the characteristic property of each nature being preserved, and
> concurring into one Person and one subsistence, not as if Christ
> were parted or divided into two persons, but one and the same Son
> and only-begotten God, Word, Lord, Jesus Christ.[38]

37. Fitzmyer, *Romans,* 485. See John 1:14: "The Word became flesh and made his
dwelling among us." C. H. Dodd has claimed that Paul was "embarrassed" over the possible negative connotations of flesh, and therefore qualified it: "Since Paul has assumed
that *all* flesh, as such, is now under the dominion of sin, he cannot say outright (as the
Fourth Evangelist could) that Christ became flesh" (Dodd, *Romans,* 119–20).

38. See Stevenson, *Creeds, Councils and Controversies,* 352–53.

Heretical movements plagued the early church, and with the Fathers we must reject any definition of the Incarnate One that would reflect a deficiency in his divine or human nature. This includes any unsound concept of kenosis that would claim that in becoming man Christ chose to lay his deity completely aside, living a perfectly obedient human life in the power of the Spirit. There are many variants of kenoticism, including some that are more orthodox in form. "It is possible," admits anti-kenoticist Donald Bloesch, "to maintain that Christ emptied himself of his divine power but not of his divine nature. His power was always available to him, but he did not choose to draw from it." Generally speaking, however, kenoticism suffers from an overly rational assessment of the divine/human dynamic at work in Christ. The mystery of the "both-and" (and, as we shall see, the "already–not yet") must be maintained in Christ's person, for the "exalted one and the humiliated one are the same. The divine attributes are not renounced by Christ but are concealed in the humiliated Christ."[39]

If Spirit Christology is prone to err by compromising the deity of Christ, Logos Christology often underestimates the human side of the Savior. Tom Smail, for instance, is one who has criticized the Chalcedonian Definition for its failure to connect the Spirit to Christ's humanity more intimately. Smail makes a good point here, because without the prior activity of the Spirit there would have been no conception, no joining of the Son to human flesh. He is also right to warn us of Logos Christology that presents a Christ so complete that there is no room for development or struggle. Yet Smail goes awry, in my opinion, when he strains to put more emphasis on Jesus' baptism and less on the incarnation. Smail celebrates Jesus' reliance on the Spirit throughout his earthly ministry, and while not denying Christ's deity at birth like some others, he believes Jesus received his messianic power more by the Spirit's anointing at his baptism than because of his innate nature as God. In promoting his baptism agenda, Smail decries:

39. Bloesch, *Jesus Christ*, 61. Bloesch notes that P. T. Forsyth was one who walked a thin but more orthodox line as a kenoticist. Citing Forsyth, Bloesch writes: "Forsyth saw the divine attributes 'not as renounced at the Incarnation but as retracted from the actual to the potential.' The kenosis 'is accompanied by a plerosis, a process of gradual reintegration through which, by genuine moral effort, Christ regained the mode of being that He had voluntarily laid aside.'"

Calvin and much classical western christology before and after him held that as *man* Jesus grew in the power of the Spirit, but that as *Son of God*, he was eternally complete and so incapable of growth. This raises insoluble problems about how the same person can both grow and mature as a man and be, at the same time, eternally perfect as Son of God. However, such problems need not arise if we understand the Father-Son relationship in the light of what happens at Jesus' baptism.[40]

I would contend in this case that Smail is another victim of the logico-casual paradigm, and that the "insoluble problems" to which he refers might be described, to borrow Pascal's phrase, as the mystery of Jesus.

It is right to defend a doctrine of Christ's humanity that maintains the integrity of his deity from birth *and* his human development and ministry in and by the Spirit. Christopher Cocksworth assesses the Logos Christology–Spirit Christology tension:

> Much of the traditional incarnational theology of the Church has implied that Jesus was able to perform miracles simply because he was God. In an attempt to correct the traditional tendency to ignore Jesus' humanity and bypass the work of the Spirit, some charismatic Christology implies that in his incarnate form the Son was forced to operate out of the Spirit's empowering because the power of his own divine being had been laid aside. While deserving credit for recovering the role of the Spirit in relation to the humanity of Christ, this view fails to recognize that the Son is *eternally* operating out of the Spirit.[41]

It is apparent that a Spirit Christology that exalts Jesus as only the model Spirit-filled person is, in the words of Gary Badcock, "no christology at all."[42] At the same time, we must beware of a Logos Christology that would ignore his vital connection to the Spirit or make light of Jesus' excruciating struggle against sin, not only in the passion but also throughout his whole earthly life. It would, as Smail has reminded us, be easy to fall into a docetist mindset—one that teaches that Jesus only *appeared* to be human. In this view the Lord was not really vulnerable at

40. Smail, *Giving Gift*, 98. While Smail is not squarely in the Spirit Christology camp, one can see Forsythian elements of kenoticism (see the note directly above) in his views on the gradual spiritual development of Jesus.

41. Cocksworth, *Holy, Holy, Holy*, 183. Emphasis mine.

42. Badcock, *Light of Truth*, 163.

all, but some kind of invincible man of steel. What does the Chalcedon formulation mean when it says that Christ was "like us in all things apart from sin"?[43] In light of the fact that Christ never sinned, how much like us could he really be? Can he really understand and relate to a humanity mired in the bog of sin?

In tackling these questions it is imperative that we return to Romans 8:3 to investigate the nuances of the Apostle's phrase "in the likeness of sinful flesh." Surely Paul has good reason for describing Christ's humanity with the more delicate, indirect phraseology "in the likeness." On why Paul does not use the more absolute expression "sinful flesh," Anders Nygren has commented:

> Paul wants to come as close to that as possible without falling into conflict with the sinlessness of Christ, of which he is absolutely certain. He comes close to the dividing line; but he does not step over it. . . . In that expression there is no hint of docetism. Christ's carnal nature was no unreality, but simple, tangible fact. He shared all our conditions. He was under the same powers of destruction.[44]

We can confidently posit, then, that by walking this "line," Paul is endeavoring to hold together Christ's assumption of our sinful nature with the fact that he did not sin. He is well aware that if Christ did not take on sinful flesh, humans cannot be thoroughly saved. Outside of a holistic doctrine of the atonement, the cross becomes a judicial or forensic transaction that "settles the books" and deals with the penalty of sin, but without dealing with the root of the problem. To put it another way, our salvation becomes something accomplished "over our heads" instead of being a victory from the depths of human need. In the doctrine of the vicarious humanity of Christ, his death and resurrection must be seen as the culmination of a lifelong struggle against the forces of sin—an inside-out overcoming by the "one mediator between God and men, the man Christ Jesus" (1 Tim 2:5). In Gregory of Nazianzus's famous words:

> For that which he has not assumed, he has not healed; but that which is united to his Godhead, is also saved. If only half Adam

---

43. This phrase is obviously rooted in Heb 4:15: "For we do not have a high priest who is unable to sympathize with our weaknesses, but we have one who has been tempted in every way, just as we are—yet was without sin."

44. Nygren, *Romans*, 315.

fell, then that which Christ assumes and saves may be half also; but if the whole of Adam fell, he must be united to the whole nature of him who was begotten, and so be saved as a whole. Let them not then begrudge our complete salvation, or clothe the savior only with bones and nerves and the portraiture of man.[45]

If Christ took on injured and not pre-fall flesh, the issue that still begs for attention is that of Christ's personal guilt. We have marked the boundaries: Christ did not sin; that is a nonnegotiable theological baseline, the abandonment of which relegates Christ to the status of (to coin a phrase) "human commensurate" instead of Savior. But to say that Christ died *for* our sins as some kind of instrumental substitute is just as damaging, for it makes him too far removed from those he is saving. By "he condemned sin in sinful man" (Rom 8:3), Paul means that God dealt with sin not simply within the fleshly sphere of human existence but more specifically within the flesh of Christ himself.[46]

For someone who has not thought through the soteriological pre-requisite of Christ's assumed humanity, remarks like those below from Colin Gunton may seem shocking, distasteful, or even offensive. Gunton writes: "This is not ready-made, perfect flesh sent down from heaven, avoiding the messiness of involvement in sin and evil. He comes 'from heaven' indeed, but only by means of a full embodiment in the matter of the fallen world he came to save"; "the material for Jesus' body comes from the common stock from which ours and that of other creatures is constructed . . . , that same corrupt matter."[47]

What makes Christ different, asserts C. E. B. Cranfield, "is not a matter of the character of his human nature (of its being not quite the same as ours), but of what He did with His human nature."[48] We can only imagine the extent to which the synapses of sin in Jesus' flesh beckoned him toward disobedience to the Father, yet the drives and impulses were resisted again and again; the Lord did not succumb. As to whether Jesus carried "original sin" in his person, we can say "yes," as long as we endorse a definition of the term that does not equate "original sin" with personal guilt. This tension is delineated by Nels Ferre: "No one, of course, can sin for anyone else; therefore 'original' sin cannot be inherited *as sin*,

---

45. In Stevenson, *Creeds, Councils and Controversies*, 90.

46. Moo, *Romans*, 480.

47. Gunton, *Christian Faith*, 100, 102.

48. Cranfield, *Romans*, 177.

but only as the occasion for sin or as the drive towards sin from within a common human nature."[49] The assumption of sin by Christ, reminds Ferre, must be understood "not in the sense that God could ever sin, certainly not even in human form, but that the human nature of Jesus shared our whole history of alienation from God."[50] Put simply, Christ was the only one in human history able to resist the drives inherent in original sin. It is via this common denominator of sinful flesh that Christ achieves maximum solidarity with Adam's descendants. And it is as the Second Adam that he is able to reverse the work of the first.

At Jesus' baptism we get a wonderful integration of Jesus as Son of God and as Son of Man, or shall we say more fittingly, Spirit-anointed Son of Man. There, as described by Colin Gunton, "John was pronouncing judgement on disobedient Israel, and it is when Jesus accepts for himself that judgement that we read of the Spirit's descent upon Him."[51] Having numbered himself with the transgressors, Jesus, "full of the Holy Spirit" (Luke 4:1),[52] is then ushered into the desert by the Spirit to face forty days of severe testing, in which he confronts and conquers sinful impulses to power and influence.[53] The victory over temptation in the wilderness certainly did not mean the end of Jesus' struggles, for it was only the beginning of several recorded years of ever-present adversity, culminating in the shadowy trial of Gethsemane and the agony of Calvary. "We must at all costs," warns Gunton, "avoid speaking of a life that is somehow immune from the struggle that marks all human life. Rather, we must realize that the whole of Jesus' life was the bearing of a cross."[54]

In a sense, Jesus' baptism is a microcosm of his incarnation and atonement, his vicarious humiliation and exaltation. Here we have an illustrative moment of Jesus first submerging himself under our sentence of sin and death and then "breaking out" by and in the Spirit. This provides a perfect segue back to Romans 8:2–3, for in returning to these

49. Ferre, *Christ and the Christian*, 90.

50. Ibid., 113–14.

51. Gunton, *Christian Faith*, 103–4.

52. After the temptations, Luke records in this same chapter Jesus' announcing of his ministry, "The Spirit of the Lord is on me" (4:18).

53. See Gunton, *Christian Faith*: "Did Jesus have 'sinful impulses'? . . . If entertaining the suggestion that he might worship the devil—seeking to attain power and influence by using the weapons of the fallen world—is a sinful impulse, then he did" (108).

54. Ibid., 102.

verses we can see how Paul encapsulates the double movement of incar-
nation/atonement in Christ:

> Through Christ Jesus the law of the Spirit of life set me free from
> the law of sin and death. For what the law was powerless to do, in
> that it was weakened by the sinful nature, God did by sending his
> own Son in the likeness of sinful man to be a sin offering. And so
> he condemned sin in sinful man. (8:2–3)

When we were powerless to meet the standard, Christ acted in our
place to present a perfect offering to the Father. This condemning of sin
was something only Christ in the Spirit could accomplish by becoming one with crooked humanity in order to bend it back straight from
within. In his vicarious obedience throughout the struggles of his life
and in his death, Christ gave us hope for change now and the guarantee
of victory in the end. C. E. B. Cranfield comments on Paul's meaning
regarding the condemnation of sin in the flesh:

> It indicates where God's "condemnation" of sin took place. It took
> place in the flesh, that is, in Christ's flesh, Christ's human nature
> . . . [And must] mean more than the pronouncing of sentence of
> condemnation. . . . That Paul had in mind Christ's death as the
> event in which the full weight of God's wrath against sin was, in
> the flesh of Christ, that is, in His human nature, so effectively
> brought to bear upon all the sin of all mankind, as to rule out its
> ever having to be brought to bear upon it in any other flesh—this
> is scarcely to be doubted. But, if we recognize that Paul believed it
> was fallen human nature which the Son of God assumed, we shall
> probably be inclined to see here also a reference to the uninter-
> mittent warfare of His whole earthly life by which He forced our
> rebellious nature to render a perfect obedience to God.[55]

A NEW ESCHATOLOGICAL FRAMEWORK FOR PRAYER

Our quest to grasp Paul's theology of prayer as grace in Romans 8 has
taken a mandatory diversion. We have been considering how what the
Spirit does on our behalf has everything to do with what Christ *has done*
in the Spirit on our behalf. In establishing a christological substructure,
we have moved well beyond the familiar humiliation-exaltation theme,
where no ontological solidarity between Christ and us is deemed neces-

---

55. Cranfield, *Romans*, 177–78.

sary, and the "work of Christ" (the cross) is thus seen in an instrumental way, *as a means* to an end. Instead, we have discovered in the doctrine of the vicarious humanity of Christ that incarnation really *means atonement*. By "vicarious," we are saying that all that Christ has done as our representative applies to us. Our salvation has been fully accomplished in Christ, that is, in his person, worked out over the course of his whole earthly life, and especially at the end. As James Torrance likes to remind us, instead of the doctor giving medicine to the diseased patient (instrumental), Christ himself becomes the patient to bring healing from within. This is the overarching double movement of grace, from which we derive the real substance of our eschatological hope and prayer life in the Spirit. As we begin a sweeping turn back toward Romans 8, it is hoped that the themes we address, some new and others revisited, will be seen in a fuller light as a result of our christological analysis.

The God-humanward and human-Godward movements in Christ's person have titanic eschatological implications for us as believers. If all that Christ has accomplished applies to us, then our lives are intimately patterned with his. When Christ was conceived and birthed from the Virgin as a man under the law by the Holy Spirit, God's war against sin was won. This does not mean that the war ceased or even that the warfare became less brutal. What it does mean is that when the King was born and the kingdom inaugurated, the ensuing battles fought by Christ in the Spirit were in a new eschatological context. In other words, because he assumed spurious, sinful flesh, Jesus had to die. Yet because he was God, he had to rise. Notes Jurgen Moltmann in this connection: "When . . . we say that it was through 'the eternal Spirit' and through 'indestructible life' that Jesus offered himself up to suffer God-forsakenness, then we are already looking beyond this death."[56]

In Christ's life on earth, then, he was the embodiment of the "already–not yet"; he is therefore the foundation of our eschatological hope and certainty. When Christ was born, struggle and ultimate victory were both inevitable; when we are born by the Spirit, the same is true for us. It is our "already" that gives us hope in our "not yet," and the Spirit

---

56. Moltmann, *Spirit of Life*, 65. Moltmann is referring to two verses in Hebrews: "How much more, then, will the blood of Christ, who through the eternal Spirit offered himself unblemished to God, cleanse our consciences from acts that lead to death, so that we may serve the living God!" (9:14); and "one who has become a priest not on the basis of a regulation as to his ancestry but on the basis of the power of an indestructible life" (7:16).

who anointed and filled Christ will be the gap-closer for us as we live simultaneously in present and future eons. "Through this Spirit," adds Christopher Cocksworth, "we participate in Christ's redeemed, messianic and eschatological humanity. The Spirit regenerates us. The Spirit empowers us. The Spirit transfigures us. All that the Spirit has completed in Christ applies to us."[57]

When Christ "grabbed on" to humanity, he sanctified it. But this sanctification was not immediate—only inevitable. Sinful nature had to be allowed to run its course, with death as its intrinsic consequence. Death took Christ as far as it could take him or any of us, but it could not hold him down. Christ emerged victorious; his resurrection is the validation that sin has no future and that "death has been swallowed up in victory" (1 Cor 15:54). That is why not only Romans 8:2–3 but even more the whole chapter of Romans 8 is the picture of the double movement of grace. I say "even more" because the phrase "condemned sin in the flesh," even when understood in more than a forensic sense, is only a condensed version of the incarnate, struggling, conquering, and ascended Christ unfolded for us in the chapter.

It is imperative that we go back to this word "struggling." A simplistic, static theology of these "dual inevitabilities" can be detrimental to believers if it engenders a callous, noncompassionate fatalism or an overrealized eschatology. To fall into those traps would be to make light of Christ's very real human struggles and in turn to misinterpret our own and others'. To know the end of the story, so to speak, should not make us smug, detached, or uncaring. If the war against sin has been won, there are still furious battles to be fought, even battles that feel like wars—battles that we are into so deeply that we cannot see the light of the big picture. Christ fought these very real battles, and so do we as we share his sufferings.

It has been said that the war against Nazi Germany was won June 6, 1944—the D-Day Invasion at Normandy. While this may be true, it is doubtful that the Allies had it in mind as a *fait accompli* at the time, certainly not those on the front lines or engaged in the Battle of the Bulge a few months later. The only legitimate basis we have for verifying the statement's truth is hindsight. To make light of some of the bloodiest fighting of the war after D-Day would be an egregious error. In the same way, how could we forget the groans of anguish in the garden or the cry

57. Cocksworth, *Holy, Holy, Holy*, 185.

of hellacious dereliction on the cross, "My God, my God, why have you forsaken me?"

In the resurrection of Christ, and in our union with him by the Spirit, we have the end in the beginning. We are heirs of the resurrection promise, a glorious reality that has yet to be fully manifested. It is also due to this union, however, that we suffer in the flesh just as he did. Returning to Romans 8:

> We are heirs—heirs of God and co-heirs with Christ, if indeed we
> share in his sufferings in order that we may also share in his glory.
> I consider that our present sufferings are not worth comparing
> with the glory that will be revealed in us. (8:17–18)

"We *are* heirs," Paul emphatically states in the present tense. The "if indeed we share in his sufferings" clause is not to be construed conditionally, as if it should be our goal to suffer, but more as an objective fact and a descriptive evidence that believers are on the right course.[58] Suffering is the road to glory. Suffering may come *because* of allegiance to Christ (persecution), or, as we noted earlier, because the Spirit of Christ in us highlights the painful disparity between the "already" and the "not yet." At the same time, reflects Douglas Moo, "there is a sense in which all the suffering of Christians is 'with Christ' inasmuch as Christ was himself subject, by virtue of his 'coming in the form of sinful flesh,' to the manifold sufferings of this world in rebellion against God."[59] Thus it comes as no surprise that to share Christ's resurrection is also to share his death. Importantly, this sharing underscores our solidarity with him, and is an intimate and participatory one, as Joseph Fitzmyer relates:

> The sufferings now endured must always be seen as a partici-
> pation in the suffering of Jesus himself, in what he has already
> suffered. Christian suffering is never an individual, lonely experi-
> ence; Jesus has suffered before, and Christian suffering is only
> the overflow of his. But through such "suffering with Christ" the
> participation in his glorification is already assured.[60]

---

58. Nygren, *Romans*, 329.

59. Moo, *Romans*, 511. Again, Moo's comment should not be seen as contrary to the more universal idea that all human suffering is suffering shared in solidarity with Immanuel.

60. Fitzmyer, *Romans*, 502.

Before going any further, let us not lose sight of the fact that everything Jesus did, including his endurance of suffering, his resistance of sinful tendencies, and the ongoing sanctification of his human nature, was done in and by the Spirit. As C. H. Dodd has observed: "Sin pressed his claim against Christ, but lost his case. Christ was not condemned; Sin was. For Christ brought into the sphere of the 'flesh' the unimpaired power of the 'Spirit.'"[61] Christ was a man of the flesh and of the Spirit, but he was able to render a perfect obedience unto the Father. Was this largely because of the Spirit? We have surveyed the dangers of easy answers to this question—to say that his obedience was generated completely by his reliance on the Spirit, or to claim that it was generated completely out of his own divinity. We certainly cannot peer into the hypostatic union to analyze the dynamic interpenetrations between his natures. Without failing to acknowledge his divine prerogatives, it serves us well to look at Christ as a man similar to us and therefore as one very dependent on his relationship with the Holy Spirit during his "already–not yet" existence. "In His life, death, resurrection and ascension," notes Colin Gunton, "is to be discerned the eschatological action of God the Spirit, who thus perfects Jesus' particular humanity in space and time."[62]

In a comparison of our spiritual experience to Christ's, then, we must note a major difference sandwiched between two major similarities. One major similarity is that in the warfare Jesus waged, he felt the pain, fear, alienation, stress, loneliness, physical torment, and enticements of the flesh. The major difference is that, while Christ experienced life the way we do and faced the same temptations, he never sinned, and the perfect obedience he offered to the Father as our representative and substitute was redemptive. The second major similarity is that the very Spirit that was available to him in his struggles is available to us. Because of what Christ has accomplished, we are no longer slaves to sin, and the Spirit enables us to resist temptation, to hold up under adversity, to be content in all circumstances, and even to change our ways.

Unfortunately, when it comes to our relationships with God, we are plagued by inconsistency. We must constantly remind one another that Christ, in and by the Spirit, has already responded in perfect obedience to the Father on our behalf and in our place. Now we are called *not* to do it ourselves, in the sense of following Christ's example, or even in the

61. Dodd, *Romans*, 120.

62. Gunton, *One*, 205.

noble sense of doing it *for* him, but to participate in what has *already* been done by Christ and what is being done in and through us by his Spirit. All of our responses to God are imperfect, although some may appear more inadequate or faithless than others, but because we are in Christ, and because by the Spirit he is in us, his uniquely faithful response is received by the Father as ours. Everything is bracketed by this grace within which our relationship to God thrives. Notice the brackets of grace ("in Christ Jesus") even around the eighth chapter of Romans: "There is now no condemnation for those who are in Christ Jesus" (8:1); "neither height nor depth, nor anything else in all creation, will be able to separate us from the love of God that is in Christ Jesus our Lord" (8:39).

We are finally ready to come back around to the topic of prayer as grace in Romans 8. At an earlier juncture we looked at prayer as being the best means of "eschatological activism." This is the obvious place to start, because it is the way chosen by Jesus and the Spirit. While we have discussed the great truth in Romans 8 of the Spirit's prayers in and for us, we have not addressed Christ's role in eschatological prayer as articulated by Paul.

> In the same way, the Spirit helps us in our weakness. We do not know what we ought to pray for, but the Spirit himself intercedes for us with groans that words cannot express. And he who searches our hearts knows the mind of the Spirit, because the Spirit intercedes for the saints in accordance with God's will. (8:26–27)

Who will bring any charge against those whom God has chosen? It is God who justifies. Who is he that condemns? Christ Jesus, who died—more than that, who was raised to life—is at the right hand of God and is also interceding for us. (8:33–34)

I have reproduced the first text, concerning the Holy Spirit, as a point of comparison with the second one. But before we can investigate the relationship of the Spirit and Christ in eschatological prayer, we must take note of Christ's exalted place at the right hand of the Father. Whereas 8:3 describes Jesus as being sent by the Father to take on fallen flesh and to provide the perfect sin offering, 8:34 captures Christ back home with the Father after his God-humanward and human-Godward movement of grace. At this stage God has in Christ reconciled the world to himself (2 Cor 5:17–18). Now that Christ is ascended in his glorified humanity, our experience of him is in and by the Spirit.

The Spirit comes to us on our side of the relationship to connect us personally to Christ. "The Holy Spirit," remarks Tom Smail, "is not the one to whom we relate but rather the one who makes the relating possible."[63] Until the Son had ascended, the Spirit could not be given by and in the name of the Son, but now the pneumatic "turning of the corner," which we have discussed, takes place. The Christ of the Spirit becomes the Spirit of Christ in our experience, as Moltmann reminds us: "Pneumatology . . . brings christology and eschatology together. There is no mediation between Christ and the kingdom of God except the present experience of the Spirit, for the Spirit is the Spirit of Christ and the living energy of the new creation of all things."[64]

The eschatological connection between the Spirit and the Son is most apparent in Paul's discussion of prayer in Romans 8. The glorified Christ is at the right hand of the Father, where he lives to make intercession for us and continues his self-offering to the Father on our behalf.[65] This is the basis for my earlier point that the ongoing vicarious humanity of Christ in heaven and the Spirit of Christ in the believer have the closest imaginable—actually, indissoluble—relationship. Tom Smail portrays the scene: "[Paul] describes two offerings of intercession that are made on behalf of the Church. The first takes place in heaven . . . , the second in the hearts of God's people. . . . Christ prays for us from a highly exalted position above us, the Spirit prays the same prayer from a position deep within us."[66] Here we have the Spirit echoing the prayers of the Son with the believer getting caught in the beneficent cross fire!

What is the meaning of this, and why would it be important for Paul to mention three separate times in such short order the idea of believers being prayed for by God? I have taken pains to show that our understanding of prayer in Romans 8 must be built on the foundation of the vicarious humanity of Christ, the judgment against sin that he put himself under on our behalf in the flesh, and the resulting salvific

63. Smail, *Giving Gift*, 61.

64. Moltmann, *Spirit of Life*, 69.

65. See Heb 7:25. This idea of the continuing priesthood of Christ is a theme in Hebrews, and although I cannot prove that Paul had this metaphor in mind here, it would certainly fit the context. Writes Tom Smail: "Prayer is the central activity of the ascended Jesus. . . . His ascension is not his retiral from his saving work; it is his entering into a new phase of it by his occupation of the place of authority at the right hand of God" (Smail, *Giving Gift*, 206).

66. Ibid., 47.

condemnation of that sin. Paul does not want us to miss this. To discuss the theology of the Spirit's prayers in and for us in a vacuum, without the vital link to Christ, could sound like spiritual wish-wash. The only reason the Holy Spirit can pray for us deep within us is because Christ himself, who sent the Spirit in his name, has plumbed the depths of the human condition. All of the Spirit's prayer must be grounded in this. The groans of the people of God and the groans of the Spirit must be connected to the groans of the incarnate Christ.

And so let us return to the passion, where we see the deepest point of Christ's agony and identification with us. There he experiences the "condescendence of the Spirit," to borrow from Moltmann. The Spirit leads and therefore accompanies Jesus; he is, continues Moltmann,

> drawn into his sufferings, and becomes his *companion* in suffering. The path the Son takes in his passion is then at the same time the path taken by the Spirit, whose strength will be proved in Jesus' weakness. . . . [The Spirit] participates in his human suffering to the point of death on the cross. . . . The Spirit binds itself to Jesus' fate, though without becoming identical to him. In this way *the Spirit of God* becomes definitively *the Spirit of Christ*, so that from that point onwards it can be called by and invoked in Christ's name.[67]

The parallel with Romans 8 is hard to miss, and that Moltmann has this exact passage in mind is even clearer in what follows:

> The Spirit does not suffer in the same way, for he is Jesus' strength in suffering, . . . in whose power Jesus can give himself vicariously "for many." In Gethsemane the divine Spirit is present and frames the Son's response: "Not my will, but thine, be done." . . . On Golgotha the Spirit suffers the suffering and death of the Son, without dying with him. So what the Spirit "experiences"—though we must not overstress the metaphor—is surely that the dying Jesus "breathes him out" and "yields him up" (Mark 15:37; stronger, John 19:30). "Of such a kind was Christ's death cry: as his senses left him and he went down to death, the Holy Spirit interceded for him, with inexpressible groanings, helping his weakness also."[68]

67. Moltmann, *Spirit of Life*, 62.

68. Ibid., 64. The last sentence is cited by Moltmann from Thus E. Vogelsang. Moltmann's theology regarding the Spirit and the cross is stimulating. He claims that "the Spirit is the transcendent side of Jesus' immanent way of suffering" (62). Certainly, while we do not say that the Spirit was crucified, or that the Spirit rose from the dead, we must be somewhat careful about approaching trinitarian dynamics surrounding the

To summarize the point colloquially, Jesus Christ and the Spirit have "been there and done that." The condescension of the Spirit of Christ to us is the most genuine and heartfelt kind, because it is grounded in the actual experience of the Son of Man. The whole scene of the disconsolate Jesus wrestling in prayer with the Father is intimate and gut-wrenching, causing one to exclaim, "How human!":

> He took Peter, James and John along with him, and he began to be deeply distressed and troubled. "My soul is overwhelmed with sorrow to the point of death," he said to them. "Stay here and keep watch." Going a little farther, he fell to the ground and prayed that if possible the hour might pass from him. "*Abba*, Father," he said, "everything is possible for you. Take this cup from me. Yet not what I will, but what you will." (Mark 14:33–36)

If with Moltmann we may interpret the Gospels through the lens of Romans 8, it is in the garden that we see the closest connection of Jesus' weakness and the Spirit at work in human prayer. And if, as is surely the case, the aligning of Jesus' groans to the will of the Father were aided and abetted by the Spirit's own, we may be sure that by grace the same comfort applies to us. To encourage us even more, this same Jesus, now glorified conqueror, is our heavenly advocate.

By his victorious re–gathering up of all humanity in his person, Jesus Christ has given us what is his very own, his special relationship with the Father. This did not happen "over our heads," as if in a heavenly bookkeeping transaction our righteousness was reckoned to us in a legal way. No, far more than a transaction, the atonement was a real exchange—"the wonderful exchange," noted John Calvin, "which, out of his measureless benevolence, he has made with us; that, becoming Son of man with us, he has made us sons of God with him; that, by his descent to earth, he has prepared an ascent to heaven for us; that, by taking on our mortality, he has conferred his immortality upon us."[69]

Because he has "brothered" us, the Holy Spirit places the "*Abba*, Father" prayer of Jesus on our lips.[70]

> For you did not receive a spirit that makes you a slave again to fear, but you received the Spirit of sonship. And by him we cry, "*Abba*,

---

death of Christ, which are shrouded in mystery. Moltmann acknowledges this with his comment "though we must not overstress the metaphor" above.

69. Calvin, *Inst.* 4.17.2, LCC 1362.

70. J. B. Torrance, *Worship, Community*, 72.

Father." The Spirit himself testifies with our spirit that we are God's children. Now if we are children, then we are heirs—heirs of God and co-heirs with Christ, if indeed we share in his sufferings in order that we may also share in his glory. (Rom 8:15–17)

CONCLUSION: THE STORY OF TWO LIKENESSES

I have saved this wonderful truth of sonship until the end because it is a concept that brings together everything we have been discussing. Jesus Christ became a man in order to give us a new eschatological identity— "son"/"daughter" of God. Having received the "Spirit of sonship," it is as eschatological children that we come to understand prayer as grace— prayer as within the larger response already made for us to the Father and still being made in us. This is what I mean by a full-orbed trinitarian theology of prayer.

As a litmus test, one may pose the question, "Why did God send his Son into the world?" If we reply, "To save us from . . . ," then we have got it only half right. We have quite possibly underestimated what Christ came to save us *for*, and this knowledge is indispensable for a healthy prayer life. James Torrance's comment on the "retrospective" and "prospective" views of salvation bears repeating: "Retrospectively, Christ came to save us from our past sin, from guilt, from judgment, from hell. But prospectively he came to bring us to sonship, to communion with God in the kingdom of God."[71] Through the humanity of Christ the Spirit folds us into the fellowship of the life of God. Christ belongs to God, and now, by the Spirit of sonship, so do we.[72] Christopher Cocksworth elaborates on this fellowship, as well as on the eschatological reality (the "already") of our new humanity:

> The Spirit not only relates us to Christ, he locates us in the Son's delight for the Father and in his joyous self-giving to the Father. We enter into the reciprocity between Father and Son and glorify the one in whom the Father is well pleased. At the same time we receive the pleasure which the Father has for the Son and we too are glorified. We are not glorified as God but we are glorified as human beings in the sense that in Christ we reach the perfection for which God created us. God's image is restored with us and amongst us.[73]

71. Ibid., 62.
72. Cocksworth, *Holy, Holy, Holy*, 182.
73. Ibid., 197.

Our new identity in Christ—*who* we are—has everything to do with *how* we pray.

In prayer we have the privilege of addressing the Father as *Abba*, a distinctive feature of Jesus' own prayers to God. This is a theme picked up by C. E. B. Cranfield in his comment on Romans 8:15b ("You received the Spirit of sonship. And by him we cry, *Abba*, Father"):

> The implication of this verse understood in its context is that it is in the believers' calling God "Father" that God's holy law is established and its "righteous requirement" (v.4 ["in order that the righteous requirements of the law might be fully met in us, who do not live according to the sinful nature but according to the Spirit"]) fulfilled, and that the whole of Christian obedience is included in this calling God "Father." The verse, in fact, states in principle everything that there is to say in the way of Christian ethics; for there is nothing more required of us than that we should do just this—with full understanding of what it means.[74]

This is an astounding truth, that as believers when we cry *Abba* we are claiming the promise that we have as sons and daughters of God. It is as if in that one word is wrapped up justification, sanctification, atonement, redemption, reconciliation, glorification—all in one package![75] In that one word is our perfect obedience and our perfect prayers, because, and only because, of our solidarity with Christ by the Spirit of sonship. As people of prayer we must be people of the indicative, knowing that God loves us not because we are good but because we are his. The imperatives then will be seen as ways of becoming what we *already* are in Christ. This is the intimacy and security that Jesus had with the Father during his earthly pilgrimage, and this is the promise for us today.

All of this leads us to the obvious question, and with this we shall draw our discussion to a close. If God loves us so much as his children and the truths espoused in Romans 8 are real, then why are so many

---

74. Cranfield, *Romans*, 184.

75. Martin Luther has contributed this classic comment on *Abba*: "This is but a little word, and yet notwithstanding it comprehendeth all things. The mouth speaketh not, but the affection of the heart speaketh after this manner. Although I be oppressed with anguish and terror on every side, and seem to be forsaken and utterly cast away from thy presence, yet am I thy child, and thou art my Father for Christ's sake: I am beloved because of the Beloved. Wherefore this little word, Father, conceived effectually in the heart, passeth all the eloquence of Demosthenes, Cicero, and of the most eloquent rhetoricians that ever were in the world" (cited in Moo, *Romans*, 503).

prayers unanswered? In other words, why are circumstances so difficult at times if the Son and the Spirit are both praying for us? This could cause one to question either the veracity of the Scripture or the effectiveness of the prayers of the Son and Spirit of God! Surely Simon Peter pondered the effectiveness of his Lord's intercession when only shortly before Simon's denials Jesus had said, "Simon, Simon, Satan has asked to sift you as wheat. But I have prayed for you, Simon, that your faith may not fail" (Luke 22:32). Perhaps the impetuous Simon was so sure of his stout defense of his Lord that in his braggadocio he missed the end of Jesus' statement: "*And when you have turned back*, strengthen your brothers" (italics mine). Jesus had the big picture in mind with Simon; there was no surprise involved for Jesus—his prayers for his disciple allowed for Simon's failings, and the goal was achieved in the end.

Romans 8, as we have seen, speaks of the Spirit praying for us in accordance with the will of God. His prayers are perfect and cannot be thwarted. The goal of his prayers is exposed two verses later:

> For those God foreknew he also predestined to be conformed to the likeness of his Son, that he might be the firstborn among many brothers. (Rom 8:29)

As sons and daughters, one of our greatest salves is to know that God is in control, that God knows what is best, and that God is transforming us by grace into the likeness of our elder brother. Our security as the beloved in Christ assures us that God will not penalize us for wrong prayers. Not even our sin and inadequacies can foil God's plans for us; somehow these are all included in his prayers for us and in us. In a beautifully trinitarian way, God is praying us over the bumps in the road to our sure destination. Tom Smail adds:

> As the Spirit takes the love and power of Christ with which he serves the Father and makes them ours, so also he takes the intercessory prayer of Christ in heaven and makes it ours here on earth. In the Spirit we pray Christ's perfect prayer with him. Christ prays for us before we pray for ourselves, but he keeps nothing to himself. He invites and enables us to participate. . . . When the Spirit prays in us and we pray in the Spirit, we are caught up into Christ's self-offering to the Father, who in response to our prayer does the creative and redemptive things that further his purposes in those for whom we pray.[76]

76. Smail, *Giving Gift*, 208.

In regard to this question of God's will, perhaps it would be most helpful to view the prayers of the Son and the Spirit together as the two hands of the potter.[77] As the clay, we are secure in the Father's hands. As the Father folds his hands in prayer, the Spirit comes around us, to our side of the relationship in the name of the glorified Christ. There he presses and even pinches us against the Son, gradually and lovingly molding us into his likeness. In the end, we become what we have already been in the mind of the potter since the beginning; we become what the Father has seen us to be all along. Admittedly, this is a very impersonal illustration of a very personal process, but it points us to the truth that God has a big-picture plan for us, and it is good. It is the gift of sonship. "He who did not spare his own Son, but gave him up for us all—how will he not also, along with him, graciously give us all things?" (Rom 8:32). Romans 8, then, is the story of two likenesses. From the Father, Christ came by the Spirit in the likeness of sinful flesh, so that we by the Spirit might be conformed to the likeness of the Father's Son. These are the movements of grace and the movements of prayer.

As we saw earlier, prayer, like our life with Christ, is not essentially about command-based performance; it is at its very core *relational*. Prayer is not about the right techniques. It is not like using a bow and arrow, where we should worry about our aim (praying for the right things in the right way) or whether there is enough tension in the string (conjuring up enough faith).[78] Fundamentally speaking, I have been pointing to prayer not as something we do but as something we experience and participate in through our fellowship with God. This concerns "receiving prayer from God before we offer it to God." As we listen, the Spirit opens us up, frees us, and begins to conform our imperfect prayers to his.[79]

It is this very thing that we observed in the drama of Gethsemane, as Christ in the Spirit gradually acquiesced to the will of the Father. Notes Gunton: "The outcome of [Christ's] prayer is that he freely, *willingly*, accepts what he believes to be his Father's will. Clearly, there are two wills involved, and one accepts the decision of the other. . . . The

---

77. See Rom 9:19–26 and Isa 64:8. The *two hands* idea is reminiscent of Irenaeus's analogy.

78. Smail, *Giving Gift*, 202.

79. Ibid., 210.

Father's will is fulfilled by the free human willing of his incarnate Son in the power of the Spirit."[80]

The stresses we face will not approach the magnitude of Gethsemane, but life is hard, and we will share our Savior's sufferings. We know that our own prayer, like our relationship with God, is only as strong as the weakest link; left to ourselves we are helpless to provide one acceptable utterance. The "reality of communion with God," remarks Karl Barth, is "beyond our competence."[81]

If we have learned anything about Paul's theology of prayer in Romans 8, it is that by grace we are saved and by grace we pray. It is within our eschatological sonship that we participate in the trinitarian life of prayer, and much of this prayer is carried out ineffably; "the prayer of the Spirit, which is first the prayer of Christ in heaven, is being offered to the Father in our hearts." Thankfully, whatever our trials and inadequacies in this "not yet" existence, we can know that "we carry prayer within us."[82] Prayer, finally, "has to do with one who is simply and solely nothing else but a 'groaner.'"[83] Where would we be, concludes Karl Barth, "if, even in prayer, grace be not the incoming of God with us for its own sake, as well as for ours also? If our ability to pray be not included within our sonship to God, within God's promise? Already it is so: . . . 'in the midst of the Devil's roarings . . . the Holy Spirit cries in our heart, *Abba*, Father!'"[84]

80. Gunton, *Christian Faith*, 109–10.

81. Barth, *Romans*, 316–17.

82. Smail, *Giving Gift*, 209–10.

83. Barth, *Holy Ghost*, 84.

84. Ibid., 86. The interior quotation is from Martin Luther, cited here by Barth.

Conclusion

This I Know

IN OUR DISCUSSION OF Barth, Bonhoeffer, and the Torrances we have described reality in terms of an ongoing dynamic, the double movement of grace. We have seen how important it is to articulate grace as a "Yes" to a "Yes," not simply a unilateral "Yes" from God to humans. Indeed, grace includes our human response and, far from belittling us or depersonalizing us, actually gives us the response-ability to freely respond by the Holy Spirit *within* the ongoing human Response of our brother Jesus Christ. As our mediator, it is Jesus Christ first and foremost who keeps faith with God, who obeys God, who worships God, who serves God, and who comprehensively substitutes for and represents all of his human brothers and sisters to the Father in all things of God. What a joy to know that Jesus Christ in a sense brackets our existence, keeping the eternal covenant of grace between God and humanity from both sides.

Of course, we are continually resisting the gift of grace by attempting to extract our actions toward God from this double movement and set them on their own ground. Our sinful minds tempt us to think in self-justifying ways, or as the branch detached from the vine, as if we were generating acts of faith, love, worship, service, and so on, from ourselves. In the preceding chapters we have noted how susceptible we can be to humanistic thinking in the areas of gospel proclamation, gospel response, obedience, and prayer.

It is easy to acknowledge that a "muscular" Christianity is a heavy yoke that leads to disillusionment and burnout. But the question inevitably arises, if in reality we are already and always preaching, responding, obeying, and praying because of our union with Christ and the Spirit, does that mean we do not have to do those things? To believe in Jesus Christ is to know that we don't *have* to do them at all—the reality doesn't change if we do or if we don't. But to believe is also to know and experience this kind of unconditional love to such an extent that we can't help but do them!

As we have learned from Barth and Bonhoeffer, it is here that we enter the freedom and joy of the obedience of Christ, he who obeyed, not to gain the Father's love, but because he knew that he was loved. In the same way, we love God because God first loved us.

There is much more to say. Questions beckon regarding epistemology, sin, the church, freedom, agency, ethics, heaven, and hell. I look forward to addressing how these issues relate to Christo-realism in subsequent publications. Of course, there are other brands of realism to contend with as well, such as Eastern Pantheism, Platonism, and various New Age constructions of reality. But only Christo-realism defines reality as existing in one dynamic person, Jesus Christ, who is our narrow way into understanding the vibrant communion and love relationship between the Triune Persons.

Through Christ we discover that which has been hidden, known variously in the New Testament as the kingdom of God (Gospels), the mystery of Christ (Paul), or eternal life (John). This ever-present Triune reality, always a dimension of human life, has been revealed in Christ, and in repentance we find ourselves there! Importantly, this is a reality that always operates by God's condescension of grace; in other words, it entails the mystery of God's union with humanity, but never as a natural or inherent part of humanity. We must always remember that grace is pure gift. And knowing God the Father of our Lord Jesus Christ is knowing the Giver of the Gift (John 17:3); it is not the same as knowing oneself.

While mentors like J. B. and T. F. Torrance, Colin Gunton, and Ray Anderson have departed in recent years, there is a new generation of enthusiastic scholars and evangelists who have benefited from their insights. Disciples are being produced who are brimful of assurance and stoked with the certainty of knowing that there is one economy of grace for believers and unbelievers alike. More evangelical models are being developed around the world reflecting a Christo-centric theology that espouses belonging before believing.

In Reality Ministries we are "helping adolescents live into the loving presence and life-changing reality of Jesus Christ." We want our adolescent friends to know that the deepest reality of their lives is God's love for them. We call the Reality Center a place with no margins, where everyone is at the center of the Father's love. Together we are relishing our belovedness in the Son. So whether it is with our friends with cognitive disabilities or with any of the other various groups we serve, our focus is on the One who is responding to God for us in spite of our limitations more than it is on our own ability to respond. We continue to find that in a worshipful, Christ-centered atmosphere, void of the pressure to respond, response flourishes! And the always-participatory nature of response should only heighten the desire in an evangelist's heart to witness that response in others.

This summer I will be preaching at our Experience Reality Camp to a group of middle-school boys and girls. I am praying that they will respond. The challenge will be to communicate the heart of the gospel of grace in a way that is relevant and accessible. T. F. Torrance used to say that a large percentage of theological questions stems from two very basic ones: What does God think of me? and Is God really like Jesus? As we have seen, the theology of grace can be magnificently nuanced, but these basic questions must always be addressed at whatever level is appropriate to the hearers. Even the most brilliant theology would be of no consequence if it could not be apprehended.

Torrance's assessment reminds me of one last story concerning his mentor. When Karl Barth was asked to summarize all that he had written about the gospel, he famously responded with the words to the song "Jesus Loves Me": "Jesus loves me, this I know, for the Bible tells me so; little ones to him belong, they are weak but he is strong." When it comes to preaching the gospel to middle-schoolers, or hearing it for myself, I would do well not to stray far from this wise and unadorned counsel of Torrance and Barth. Come, Creator Spirit!

Epilogue

I am weak and needy
And cannot live
Lest my life in you is hid
Take my burdens
And my stress
Fill my anxious soul with rest
Live your life through me I pray
Let your joy be mine today

—Jeff McSwain, during a dark time at St. Andrews, 2001

Bibliography

Anderson, Ray S., ed. *Theological Foundations for Ministry: Selected Readings for a Theology of the Church in Ministry*. Edinburgh: T. & T. Clark, 1979.

Badcock, Gary. *Light of Truth and Fire of Love: A Theology of the Holy Spirit*. Grand Rapids: Eerdmans, 1997.

Barrett, C. K. *Paul: An Introduction to His Thought*. Louisville: Westminster, 1994.

Barth, Karl. "All." In *Deliverance to the Captives*, 85–92.

———. "By Grace You Have Been Saved." In *Deliverance to the Captives*, 35–42.

———. *Call for God*. Translated by A. T. Mackay. London: SCM, 1967.

———. *Church Dogmatics*. Edited by G. W. Bromiley and T. F. Torrance. Translated by G. T. Thomson et al. Edinburgh: T. & T. Clark, 1936–77.

———. *Deliverance to the Captives*. Translated by Marguerite Wieser. London: SCM, 1961.

———. *Dogmatics in Outline*. New York: Harper & Row, 1959.

———. *The Epistle to the Romans*. Translated by Edwyn C. Hoskyns. London: Oxford University Press, 1933.

———. *The Holy Ghost and the Christian Life*. Translated by R. Birch Hoyle. London: Frederick Muller, 1938.

———. "Teach Us to Number Our Days." In *Deliverance to the Captives*, 117–125.

———. "You May." In *Call for God*, 19–27.

Bauckham, Richard. *God Crucified: Monotheism and Christology in the New Testament*. Carlisle: Paternoster, 1998.

Bethge, Eberhard. *Costly Grace: An Illustrated Biography of Dietrich Bonhoeffer*. Translated by Rosaleen Ockenden. San Francisco: Harper & Row, 1979.

———. *Dietrich Bonhoeffer: Theologian, Christian, Contemporary*. Translated by Eric Mosbacher et al. London: Collins, 1970.

Bloesch, Donald G. *Jesus Christ: Savior and Lord*. Carlisle: Paternoster, 1997.

Bonhoeffer, Dietrich. *Christology*. Translated by John Bowden. London: Collins, 1966.

———. *The Cost of Discipleship*. Translated by R. H. Fuller. London: SCM, 1959.

———. *Ethics*. Edited by Eberhard Bethge. Translated by Neville Horton Smith. London: SCM, 1955.

———. *Letters and Papers from Prison*. Edited by Eberhard Bethge. Translated by Reginald Fuller et al. London: SCM, 1971.

Campbell, Douglas. *The Rhetoric of Righteousness in Romans 3:21-26*. JSNTSup 65. Sheffield: JSOT Press, 1992.

Cocksworth, Christopher. *Holy, Holy, Holy: Worshipping the Trinitarian God*. London: Darton, Longman & Todd, 1997.

Cranfield, C. E. B. *Romans: A Shorter Commentary*. Grand Rapids: Eerdmans, 1985.

Dodd, C. H. *The Epistle of Paul to the Romans*. London: Hodder & Stoughton, 1937.

Dunn, James D. G. *Christology*. Vol. 1 of *The Christ and the Spirit*. Edinburgh: T. & T. Clark, 1998.

———. *Jesus and the Spirit*. Grand Rapids: Eerdmans, 1997.

———. "Spirit Speech: Reflections on Romans 8:12–27." In *Romans and the People of God: Essays in Honor of Gordon D. Fee on the Occasion of His 65th Birthday*, edited by Sven K. Soderlund and N. T. Wright, 82–91. Grand Rapids: Eerdmans, 1999.

Feil, Ernst. *The Theology of Dietrich Bonhoeffer*. Translated by Martin Rumscheidt. Philadelphia: Fortress, 1985.

Fee, Gordon. *God's Empowering Presence: The Holy Spirit in the Letters of Paul*. Peabody: Hendrickson, 1994.

———. *Paul, the Spirit, and the People of God*. Peabody: Hendrickson, 1996.

Ferre, Nels F. S. *Christ and the Christian*. London: Collins, 1958.

Fitzmyer, Joseph A. *Romans*. London: Geoffrey Chapman, 1993.

Godsey, John. *The Theology of Dietrich Bonhoeffer*. London: SCM, 1960.

Green, Clifford J. *Bonhoeffer: A Theology of Sociality*. Grand Rapids: Eerdmans, 1999.

Gunton, Colin. *The Christian Faith: An Introduction to Christian Doctrine*. London: Blackwell, 2001.

———. *The One, the Three, and the Many*. Cambridge: Cambridge University Press, 1996.

Hart, Trevor. *Faith Thinking: The Dynamics of Christian Theology*. Downers Grove: InterVarsity, 1995.

———. "Humankind in Christ and Christ in Humankind: Salvation as Participation in Our Substitute in the Theology of John Calvin." *SJT* 42 (1989) 67–84.

———. "Irenaeus, Recapitulation and Physical Redemption." In *Christ in Our Place: The Humanity of God in Christ for the Reconciliation of the World: Essays Presented to James Torrance*, edited by Trevor Hart and Daniel Thimell, 152–81. Exeter: Paternoster, 1989.

Hart, Trevor, and Richard Bauckham. *Hope against Hope: Christian Eschatology in Contemporary Context*. London: Darton, Longman & Todd, 1999.

Hays, Richard B. "PISTIS and Pauline Christology: What Is at Stake?" In *SBL 1991 Seminar Papers*, edited by E. H. Lovering Jr., 714–29. Atlanta: Scholars Press, 1991.

Hunsinger, George. *How to Read Karl Barth: The Shape of His Theology*. Oxford: Oxford University Press, 1991.

Jeremias, Joachim. *The Prayers of Jesus*. Norwich: SCM, 1967.

Jones, L. Gregory. *Embodying Forgiveness: A Theological Analysis*. Grand Rapids: Eerdmans, 1995.

Kelly, Geoffrey B. *Liberating Faith: Bonhoeffer's Message for Today*. Minneapolis: Augsburg, 1984.

Marsh, Charles. *Reclaiming Dietrich Bonhoeffer: The Promise of His Theology*. Oxford: Oxford University Press, 1994.

Moltmann, Jurgen. *The Spirit of Life: A Universal Affirmation*. London: SCM, 1992.

Moo, Douglas. *The Epistle to the Romans*. Grand Rapids: Eerdmans, 1996.

Mortimer, Ernest. *Blaise Pascal: The Life and Work of a Realist*. London: Methuen, 1959.

Moser, Carl. "The Greatest Possible Blessing: Calvin and Deification." *SJT* 55 (2002) 36–57.

Nygren, Anders. *Commentary on Romans*. Translated by Carl C. Rasmussen. London: SCM, 1952.

Ott, Heinrich. *Reality and Faith: The Theological Legacy of Dietrich Bonhoeffer*. Translated by Alexa Morrison. Philadelphia: Fortress, 1972.

Pangritz, Andreas. *Karl Barth in the Theology of Dietrich Bonhoeffer*. Translated by Barbara and Martin Rumscheidt. Grand Rapids: Eerdmans, 2000.

Phillips, John. *The Form of Christ in the World*. London: Collins, 1967.

Rasmussen, Larry. *Dietrich Bonhoeffer: His Significance for North Americans*. Minneapolis: Fortress, 1990.

Robertson, Edwin H. "Bonhoeffer's Christology." In *Christology*, by Dietrich Bonhoeffer, 9–24. London: Collins, 1966.

Smail, Tom. *The Giving Gift: The Holy Spirit in Person*. London: Hodder & Stoughton, 1988.

Stevenson, J. *Creeds, Councils and Controversies*. London: SPCK, 1989.

Tinsley, E. J. *Dietrich Bonhoeffer*. Modern Theology 5. London: Epworth, 1973.

Torrance, Alan. "The Trinity." In *The Cambridge Companion to Karl Barth*, edited by John Webster, 72–91. Cambridge: Cambridge University Press, 2000.

Torrance, James B. "The Concept of Federal Theology—Was Calvin a Federal Theologian?" *Calvinus Sacrae Scripturae Professor: Calvin as Confessor of Holy Scripture*, edited by Wilhelm H. Neuser, 15–39. Grand Rapids: Eerdmans, 1994.

———. "The Covenant Concept in Scottish Theology and Politics and Its Legacy." *SJT* 34 (1981) 224–43.

———. "Covenant or Contract? A Study of the Theological Background of Worship in Seventeenth-Century Scotland." *SJT* 23 (1970) 51–76.

———. "The Doctrine of the Trinity in Our Contemporary Situation." In *The Forgotten Trinity*, edited by Alasdair I. C. Heron, 3–17. London: Inter-Church, 1991.

———. "The Incarnation and Limited Atonement." *EvQ* 55 (1983) 83–94.

———. "Interpreting the Word by the Light of Christ or the Light of Nature? Calvin, Calvinism, and Barth." In *Calviniana*, edited by Robert Schnucker, 255–67. Kirksville, MO: Sixteenth Century Journal, 1988.

———. "The Place of Christ in Worship." In Anderson, *Theological Foundations for Ministry*, 348–69.

———. "The Priesthood of Jesus: A Study in the Doctrine of the Atonement." In *Essays in Christology for Karl Barth*, edited by T. H. L. Parker, 155–73. London: Lutterworth, 1956.

———. "Strengths and Weaknesses of the Westminster Theology." In *The Westminster Confession in the Church Today*, edited by Alasdair I. C. Heron, 40–54. Edinburgh: St. Andrews, 1982.

———. "The Vicarious Humanity and Priesthood of Christ in the Theology of John Calvin." In *Calvinus Ecclesiae Doctor*, edited by Wilhelm H. Neuser, 69–84. Kampen: Kok, 1978.

———. *Worship, Community, and the Triune God of Grace*. Carlisle: Paternoster, 1996.

Torrance, Thomas F. "The Atonement. The Singularity of Christ and the Finality of the Cross: The Atonement and Moral Order." In *Universalism and the Doctrine of Hell*, edited by Nigel M. de S. Cameron, 225–56. Carlisle: Paternoster, 1992.

———. "Cheap and Costly Grace." *BQ* 22 (1968) 290–311.

———. *The Christian Frame of Mind*. Edinburgh: Handsel, 1985.

———. *Christian Theology and Scientific Culture*. Belfast: Christian Journals, 1980.

———. "The Church in the New Era of Scientific and Cosmological Change." In Anderson, *Theological Foundations for Ministry*, 752–76.

―――. *Conflict and Agreement in the Church.* 2 vols. London: Lutterworth, 1959.

―――. "Deposit of Faith." *SJT* 36 (1983) 1–28.

―――.. *Divine and Contingent Order.* Oxford: Oxford University Press, 1981.

―――. *The Doctrine of Grace in the Apostolic Fathers.* Edinburgh: Oliver & Boyd, 1948.

―――. The Eclipse of God." *BQ* 22 (1967) 194–214.

―――. *God and Rationality.* London: Oxford University Press, 1971.

―――. "The Goodness and Dignity of Man in the Christian Tradition." *ModT* 4 (1988) 309–22.

―――. *The Ground and Grammar of Theology.* Belfast: Christian Journals, 1980.

―――. Introduction to *The Incarnation: Ecumenical Studies in the Nicene-Constantinopolitan Creed A.D. 381*, edited by Thomas F. Torrance. Edinburgh: Handsel, 1981.

―――. *Karl Barth: An Introduction to His Early Theology, 1910–1931.* Edinburgh: T. & T. Clark, 1962.

―――. *Karl Barth: Biblical and Evangelical Theologian.* Edinburgh: T. & T. Clark, 1990.

―――. *The Mediation of Christ.* Rev. ed. Colorado Springs: Helmers & Howard, 1992.

―――. "One Aspect of the Biblical Conception of Faith." *ExpTim* 68 (1956–57) 111–14.

―――. "A Pilgrimage in the School of Christ: An Interview with Thomas F. Torrance." By I. John Hesselink. *RefR* 38 (1984) 47–64.

―――. "The Place of Christology in Biblical and Dogmatic Theology." In *Essays on Christology for Karl Barth*, edited by T. H. L. Parker, 11–37. London: Lutterworth, 1956.

―――. *Preaching Christ Today: The Gospel and Scientific Thinking.* Grand Rapids: Eerdmans, 1994.

―――. "The Reconciliation of Mind: A Theological Meditation upon the Teaching of St. Paul." In *Theology in the Service of the Church*, edited by Wallace M. Alston Jr., 196–204. Grand Rapids: Eerdmans, 2000.

―――. *Royal Priesthood.* Edinburgh: Oliver & Boyd, 1955.

―――. "Service in Jesus Christ." In *Service in Christ*, edited by James I. McCord and T. H. L. Parker, 1–16. London: Epworth, 1966.

―――. "The Soul and Person in Theological Perspective." In *Religion, Reason and the Self, Essays in Honour of Hywel D. Lewis*, edited by Stewart R. Sutherland and T. A. Roberts, 103–18. Cardiff: University of Wales Press, 1989.

―――. *Space, Time and Incarnation.* London: Oxford University Press, 1969.

―――. *Space, Time and Resurrection.* Edinburgh: T. & T. Clark, 1976.

―――. *Theology in Reconciliation: Essays Towards Evangelical and Catholic Unity in East and West.* London: Geoffrey Chapman, 1975.

―――. *Theology in Reconstruction.* London: SCM, 1965.

―――. *The Trinitarian Faith: The Evangelical Theology of the Ancient Catholic Church.* Edinburgh: T. & T. Clark, 1995.